Balance Breakthrough:

A Practical Guide for Busy Professionals to Take Charge of Their Work, Life, and Well-being

Daniela Wolfe LMSW

Table of Contents

INTRODUCTION

In 2017, a friend invited me to an all-day wellness event. I had never been to one before, but figured a day filled with yoga, boot camp workouts, healthy food, and inspirational speakers had to be good for me.

"Sure, why not?" I said to my friend, and packed my bag.

The venue was packed to the rafters, with only a couple of centimeters between my yoga mat and the person next to me. I'm not gonna lie—I was initially a little uncomfortable being so close to that many people, but no one else seemed to mind, and the event had a calm/chill vibe.

The day did not disappoint. The boot camp class challenged me physically, the yoga calmed me, and the speakers inspired me. One powerful yoga class even made me cry—a veteran shared how he lost his legs and helped others overcome their own challenges.

When I left the event, I knew I wanted to feel that same sense of connection and like-mindedness to others, and surround myself with people achieving a higher purpose every day.

The spark I felt that day began my entrepreneurial journey. Even though I didn't create my actual business till years later, the seed was planted.

At that time, I had been a social worker for almost twenty years, and my kids required a lot of my time. The idea of starting a business sounded exciting but also daunting, unpredictable, and downright scary.

But I couldn't stop thinking about it.

At one point, a coworker and I talked about doing something together and even went as far as outlining a business plan and recording a couple of podcast episodes. But just like trying to hop into a game of double-Dutch ropes, the timing wasn't right, and we stalled.

I had been on my own self-care journey for a couple of years while working on coming out of burnout after a divorce. (I share more about this in the next chapter.) As I made changes in my own life, many women gravitated toward me as they had babies, got divorced, took care of elderly parents, and navigated other weighty life events.

They would ask, "How are you managing it all? How do *I* find some of what you've been able to do?" They saw me making more time for myself, going to the gym, and showing up happier and less stressed and irritable.

They also excitedly shared things they did for themselves because of something I said. I realized so many women are looking for validation and permission to step back from the day-to-day hustle without judgment or guilt and to take time for themselves.

Women were contacting me so often that in January 2020, I knew I needed to make my business dreams real. With the help of the small business development center at a local college and a business coach, "Best D Life, LLC" was born, allowing me to help more individuals, business owners, and their employees create a lifestyle grounded in a healthy work/life balance.

Reading this book about burnout prevention and self-care doesn't make you (or me) immune to stress, frustration, or life's challenges. It does mean you can develop an awareness, habits, and practices to help you change how you react and respond to situations.

This book isn't *just* about science and strategies. It's about creating a way of life and a lifestyle that you love!

Nobody plans to burn out.

What starts as ambition, motivation, and passion can slowly change to feeling overwhelmed and resentful, causing you to wake up and see yourself acting in ways that you hadn't planned.

You may end the day exhausted, feeling like you've been running nonstop all day but still have a mile-long to-do list. You may also feel guilty about taking time for yourself and not being there for your kids, spouse, partner, or aging parents. You feel stressed, overwhelmed, and like you've lost yourself while being there for everyone else.

While the sources and causes of burnout can vary, everyone can adopt my actionable, attainable strategies.

I wrote this book for *you* if you're an overwhelmed, stressed, constantly on-the-go professional who never has time for yourself. Deep down, do you want to accomplish one (or all) of the following?:

- Let go of the feeling that you must always be busy.
- Create space for yourself (even if you feel you don't have the time).
- Stop the grind.
- Feel a sense of accomplishment at the end of the day.
- Create space and energy for yourself and your family.
- Invest in your personal development.
- Live life as the best version of yourself—not the "what's left over" version.
- Stop clinging to the same old behaviors that got you to this point.

You thrive on setting and achieving ambitious goals, seeking opportunities, advancing in your career, or building your own business and making a significant impact.

Excellence is not just a goal; it's a way of life. Quality work and impeccable standards are non-negotiable. Amid the hustle, though, you crave a harmonious work-life balance because you know that true success goes far beyond the workplace.

You value wellness and you recognize the importance of holistic well-being, from physical health to mental resilience, but you struggle with balancing the many facets of your life. You feel you have either hit burnout (or are on the brink). You know this isn't who you are. You're not living your life how you envisioned it.

My promise to you is that by the end of this book, you'll know the different ways burnout can show up, and you'll know how to add more work-life balance into your days using mindset, time planning, and daily self-care practices.

My goal is to educate, motivate, and make it easy for you to take action *before* you hit the place I reached. If you've already experienced burnout (no judgment if you have!), I want to give you the support you need to get out of there. Think of this as a combination of a workshop, masterclass, and life-changing guide all in one, giving you access to the framework and guidance I've used for myself and my clients.

This book contains two parts:

- **Part 1** is a broad overview of burnout (what we're trying to avoid), then insight into mental fitness and work-life balance (in other words, the functions that build our resilience and make our lives better).
- **Part 2** is where the action happens—the "how-to" section. I provide the framework I use with my clients and myself, called the Exhausted to Empowered Formula. It consists of three pillars: Mindset, Time Planning, and Self-Care, which, when practiced and strengthened incrementally, lead to subtle but powerful changes.

I'll provide you with some self-assessments and action steps in each chapter. You don't need to do every single one or do them perfectly. Give yourself grace while finding what works for you. I invite you to mess up, customize the steps, and make them yours.

Remember that preventing burnout and finding a balance between work and life is all about your own individual mindset, time management, and self-care. It's not just a checklist; it's a way of living that empowers you to thrive. By embracing these principles, you'll unlock the potential for a fulfilling and joyful life journey.

Here's to crafting a life where you feel present, energized, purposeful, and truly alive!

PART 1
Navigating Roadblocks

In the past, I put self-care on my back burner. I saw it as an extravagance, rather than a daily necessity. Unfortunately, I had to burn out and hit bottom before I recognized how important it is to take care of myself, not only for my own well-being, but also for everyone around me.

I wish I could go back to my twenty-year-old self and tell her that trying to make everyone happy wouldn't help her achieve more love, happiness, or success; that losing herself while serving everyone else was actually selfish because it robbed others of the best parts of her.

A 2023 study by Advanced Dermatology states that approximately 73% of men and women report wishing for more self-care in their lives. This statistic highlights the universal need for everyone to prioritize well-being and take proactive steps to maintain a healthy life balance.

I know it can be hard to simplify and feel comfortable doing less, especially when we've been taught that hustling and working hard is the only way to be successful. But what are the consequences if we don't? (I'll cover them more in depth in each chapter.)

I don't believe there's only one way to practice self-care. I also don't believe that you have to do it quietly and calmly. Or that you have to do it alone, separate from the rest of your life. Self-care can be loud and full of laughter; you can do it with your family and friends. You can implement real, simple, practical, and transformational self-care *every single day*.

Chapter 1

The Burnout Breakdown

"Burnout is a symptom of living a life that is out of alignment with your values."

— *Sunita Raghavan*

Burnout is like a chip in your windshield—it may start small and seem like no big deal. You might even forget it's there because you've become used to it as part of your "norm." But just like a chip, it can become a larger crack that spans your entire view, affecting all the other areas of your life.

One of my clients shared how burnout started for her. She said, "It started with just an email here or there after work or on the weekend, and pretty soon, I was spending many extra hours outside of work answering emails—it became what my boss and clients *expected*."

Do you answer emails during non-work hours, too?

Unfortunately, burnout is a huge problem in modern workplaces and society. In fact, burnout is so common that the World Health Organization (WHO) has recognized it as an occupational phenomenon.

What is Burnout, Exactly?

Everybody talks about burnout, but *what is it*?

Burnout is a state of emotional, physical, and mental exhaustion that can result from prolonged periods of stress or overwork. It can happen to anyone at any age, but can be more common among people who are overachievers with perfectionist tendencies. And just like that crack in your windshield, when left unchecked, it can spread and negatively impact your physical, emotional, and mental health.

A 2023 report by Zippia states:

- 89% of workers have experienced burnout within the past year.
- 77% of employees have experienced feelings of burnout at their current job.
- 21% of workers say their company does not offer any program to help alleviate burnout.

A report by Indeed states that even the most committed employees aren't protected from symptoms of burnout. So the lesson here is that if you want yourself or others to function at their best, it's critical to regularly check in on their well-being and create a culture (not a one-and-done presentation) to systematically address burnout all year long.

Burnout is serious. You can't just power through it, and it doesn't just go away on its own. Burnout isn't about being lazy or unmotivated. It occurs when we push ourselves too hard for too long, without taking time to rest and recharge.

It's easy to get excited about the results of your efforts, no matter how big or small:

- "I just finished my first book!"
- "I made my first million!"
- "I got promoted!"

But once you reach that milestone, you might feel it's time to put a little more effort into the next one. And the next one. And the next one. Before you know it, you've spent years of your life in constant pursuit of external goals, lost time with friends and family, and your kids have grown up in the blink of an eye. Even scarier, without those outside achievements, you may no longer *know who you are*.

If you're experiencing burnout, you might be tempted to work harder, but that's not the solution, and in fact, it may actually make things worse.

I know, because I've been there myself.

I've been a full-time social worker for the last twenty-seven years and mom to two kids. Though they're older now, I know how it feels to be overwhelmed, stressed, and frustrated, running everyone around to sports practices and school events, trying to keep the house clean, cooking dinner, working, fitting in some time for myself, and maybe trying to exercise once in a while. It was hard to find a way to balance it all.

When my kids were four years old and six months old, I went through a divorce. I tried to manage everything on my own, and, unfortunately, wasn't great at asking for help. I found myself irritable and seemed to snap at my kids all the time. I was burned out, frustrated, and overwhelmed.

My personal breaking point came about five months after I had been on my own with the kids. A surprise ice storm in early October brought down tree limbs and power lines, and we were without power for five days.

We slept in front of the fireplace to stay warm, living by candlelight, and I hoped we had enough food until we could get to a grocery store. I had to bail out my sump pump with a bucket several times a day to keep my basement from flooding. On one of my trips outside with a bucket, I broke down into tears.

In that instant, I felt like I was failing my kids and myself. At that moment, I realized I wasn't living the life I wanted to lead. I wasn't becoming the person I wanted my kids to know. I felt a sense of despair that went far deeper than dealing with a flooded basement.

So I started to practice what I preached to my social work clients and found ways to fit in different strategies, habits, and routines, and intentionally changed my focus, mindset, and my life. Luckily, like that crack in the windshield, I realized that I could fix what was wrong.

Changes didn't come overnight. They happened because I implemented them intentionally, across different areas, so I could feel like a good mom, worker, friend, and partner.

I started small, with a daily gratitude practice. In a blank journal, I listed three things I was grateful for each day. They weren't necessarily "big" things. Maybe the sun was out that day, or I drank my favorite banana smoothie, or someone held the door for me— just simple moments that brought a smile to my face.

I began using the free childcare service at the grocery store and the gym. While it didn't make things instantly perfect and I had to work through some "taking-time-away-from-my-kids" guilt, it helped me find a bit of balance and happiness.

I found firsthand that self-care can help you be happy, give more to your job, your family, and make a difference in others' lives. I've seen that by empowering women to make those changes in their lives (instead of pushing a rigid, multi-step process on them), they can find happiness and balance. I'm passionate about helping others understand that taking care of themselves is *not* a luxury and *not* selfish—it's a necessity.

If you're thinking, "I'm not a parent, so I can't relate," or "I'm not going through a divorce, so this has nothing to do with me," keep this in mind:

Unfortunately, burnout doesn't discriminate.

Burnout is not just about avoiding immediate discomfort.

It's an investment in your health, career longevity, relationships, and overall life satisfaction. It's about taking a proactive approach to creating a lifestyle that you love and are excited to wake up to each day.

Are You at Risk for Burnout?

Here are some red flags to watch for:

- Feeling constantly exhausted or drained (even after a full night's sleep)
- Losing interest in activities that used to excite you
- Feeling overwhelmed, like you're drowning in your work or personal responsibilities, or feeling like you don't have control over your life
- Increased cynicism or negativity
- Decreased productivity, such as finding it hard to get work done or making more mistakes than usual
- Physical symptoms, such as headaches, stomach problems, or a weakened immune system

Now, I know we all experience some of these symptoms from time to time, but understanding all the symptoms and how often they occur can help motivate you to take action. I'll cover the actions you'll need to take in Part 2.

Are You Already There?

No one goes into their job, relationship, parenthood, etc., planning to experience burnout.

In my early twenties, I was *so* excited to finish college. I had done several internships and was ready to get to work with clients in my field and make an impact in the world. Unfortunately, the more seasoned employees in my field met my enthusiasm with cynicism or apathy.

When I heard them say things like, "Good luck lasting ten years in this job, kid. You'll get eaten alive," I'd think, *"That's crazy—I'll never get burned out helping people—I just love it so much!"*

I assumed "those" people were generally negative and miserable, and that I would never end up like that.

I had also never heard of compassion fatigue, which is a form of traumatic stress resulting from repeated exposure to traumatized individuals. If not addressed, it can also lead to burnout.

My background as a social worker helped me recognize when I began to think negatively like my more seasoned colleagues.

It was a wake up call.

When you're in the middle of your day-to-day life, with all its chaos and expectations, you might not see the real impact of your stressors, mindset, and choices.

If you're wondering what you should look for in your own life, here are some additional hints as to what burnout can look like.

Loss of Fulfillment

Loss of fulfillment means you feel what you're doing each day doesn't make a difference or it no longer brings you joy. This can happen at work, at home, or both.

At work, loss of fulfillment can come from heavy workloads, lack of control over your job (whether it's your schedule or actual work duties), and inadequate support for the tasks asked of you.

When you experience this for years, it may show up as exhaustion, cynicism, and reduced effectiveness or productivity in your work. You may also experience physical and mental health issues, such as headaches, anxiety, and depression.

Loss of fulfillment at home is a feeling of being overwhelmed by the demands of daily life, such as managing day-to-day household responsibilities, caring for family members (if you have young kids or aging parents), and balancing your own personal needs with the needs of everyone else around you. It can lead to emotional and physical exhaustion, feelings of detachment, or cynicism toward your family or home life.

All names and identifying details changed for privacy.

Sarah had always been passionate about her work in education. She loved the creativity involved in crafting lessons and the thrill of seeing individuals succeed. But after several years in the same role, something started to shift. She began to feel a sense of emptiness, even as she achieved professional success.

It started with small things. Sarah noticed she was dragging herself out of bed in the mornings. Meetings that used to energize her felt draining, and she caught herself daydreaming about a life that wasn't centered around her job.

She realized she had lost fulfillment. The work she once loved no longer felt meaningful. She realized she was going through the motions, doing what was expected of her, but the joy and purpose that had driven her were gone.

When Sarah came to me, she was frustrated and confused. She couldn't understand how she'd met all the goals she had set in college, and yet felt so disconnected from her work.

We started exploring what had changed for her and the values and passions she had grown into that her current role no longer satisfied. Sarah began to explore opportunities within her company that would allow her to work on projects that aligned with her desire to make a difference. Eventually, she transitioned into a role focused on social impact marketing, where she could combine her skills with her passion for helping others.

Over time, Sarah began to regain her sense of purpose and fulfillment at work. She went from feeling lost and disconnected to being re-energized and excited about the impact she was making through work.

Detachment

Detachment means feeling disconnected from your emotions, thoughts, or physical sensations, which can lead to a sense of numbness or aloofness from your work or personal life, making it difficult to stay engaged or motivated.

You may also feel emotionally distant from others, which might manifest itself in a lack of empathy or interest in what's happening in the lives of those around you. Lack of empathy can make it difficult to maintain healthy relationships or provide effective care for your loved ones.

Mark was an accountant at a big firm. He had always been the go-to guy on his team—sharp, reliable, and dedicated. For years, Mark took pride in his work, staying late to solve complex problems and always pushing himself.

As Mark's responsibilities grew, he found himself in endless meetings, managing junior staff members, and dealing with the pressure of tight deadlines. The work that once excited him started to feel like a never-ending grind.

Mark began to notice changes in himself. He'd sit at his desk, staring at his computer screen, unable to focus. Tasks that used to challenge him felt monotonous, and he started avoiding projects that required creative thinking. His usual enthusiasm faded, and he found himself withdrawing from team interactions.

One day, during a meeting, his manager asked for his input. Mark realized he hadn't even been listening—his mind was elsewhere. He felt detached, as if he were just going through the motions, disconnected from the work and the people around him.

I worked with him to identify the underlying causes of his detachment. Mark realized that he had lost sight of why he loved accounting in the first place. The constant pressure to perform and the shift from doing hands-on work to managing others had left him feeling disconnected.

To help him reconnect, we explored ways to reintroduce elements of his work that he found fulfilling. Mark started blocking out time to work on client projects, rediscovering his passion for problem-solving. He also worked on setting boundaries at work, cutting down on unnecessary meetings, and delegating tasks that didn't align with his strengths or interests.

Gradually, Mark began to feel more engaged. He reconnected with his team, taking the time to mentor junior developers in a way that reignited his own interests. While the pressures of his job didn't disappear, Mark's renewed focus on what he truly enjoyed helped him overcome the detachment he'd been feeling.

Recognizing these symptoms can help you take steps to manage them effectively, such as practicing stress-reduction techniques, prioritizing self-care, and seeking support from mental health professionals or trusted individuals.

Burnout Myths

People often assume burnout comes from a negative experience, like a terrible boss, job experience, or a bad relationship. But it can also result from something we're passionate about or want to spend our time working on, such as being with our kids, a relationship, or even a personal business.

When we're more personally invested in these areas, whether emotionally or financially, we tend to ride the highs and lows that can come from them in a more profound way.

It's also common to isolate ourselves in our passions. I remember chatting with a friend who shared that talking with me was her first adult conversation in four days because she had been spending so much time with her kids.

Personality Traits: Could Yours Lead to Burnout?

Many of us believe stereotypes about what we think burnout looks like. It's not just about feeling tired, overwhelmed, and fatigued. Let's bust this old myth wide open!

When we hear the word "burnout," many of us conjure up an image of someone who looks completely frazzled, exhausted, and on the verge of a breakdown. But here's the scoop, friends: *Burnout isn't always that obvious.* In fact, burnout is like a sneaky ninja that creeps up on you when you least expect it.

Crazy, huh?

Let's shine a light on some of the things we may not even realize we're doing to trigger this exhausting phenomenon.

It's not just outside situations that can cause burnout. Sometimes, it's how we respond that stops us from living the kind of life we want.

I want you to do a little self-assessment as you read the following personality traits. Do any of them sound familiar? When you become conscious of them, you can intentionally work on and prevent your personality traits from leading to burnout.

The Perfectionist

Perfectionists strive for perfection in everything they do. They never cut themselves any slack, and they're super critical of themselves.

Surprise! A relentless pursuit of excellence can lead straight to burnout.

What are some of the signs?

- Unrealistic standards (believing everything must be flawless)
- Chronic stress from the fear of making mistakes or falling short of perfection
- Long hours overworking and neglecting self-care, sleep, and relaxation
- All-or-nothing thinking—it's either perfection or failure
- Self-criticism (being your own harshest critic)
- Procrastination (from a fear of not completing tasks perfectly), causing increased stress due to completing jobs at the last minute
- Difficulty delegating, believing no one else can meet your standards
- Social isolation, prioritizing work over relationships

- Lack of enjoyment of your accomplishments because you're too focused on perceived flaws

In essence, perfectionism can create a vicious cycle of high standards, chronic stress, and self-criticism, which can ultimately result in burnout.

The "I-Can-Do-It-All" Master (This Was Me!)

You're the go-to person for everyone's problems, the one who manages a million tasks. The more you take on, the closer you get to burnout, because things start falling apart. But trying to be a superhero can lead to stress, exhaustion, and, you guessed it, burnout.

"I-Can-Do-it-All" Masters signs include:

- Overloading by taking on multiple roles and responsibilities without recognizing limits
- Constant juggling within and between roles
- Perfectionism in all roles, which can lead to chronic stress
- Lack of self-care when trying to be superhuman, with little time for rest, relaxation, and personal well-being
- Blurring boundaries between work, family, and personal life
- Difficulty asking for help (believing you should handle everything yourself)
- Role conflict, where the expectations of one role clash with another
- Emotional exhaustion
- Social isolation (putting needs and social life on hold to fulfill all roles)

Take a vital step toward preserving well-being and preventing burnout: Recognize that it's okay not to be "super" all the time. It's a vital step toward preserving well-being and preventing burnout.

The "Lack of Priorities" Person

Some people have difficulty setting priorities and believe everything is urgent and important, but it's *not*! Failing to set clear boundaries in our personal and professional lives can lead to a chaotic existence and keep us from feeling like we have work/life balance.

Blurred boundaries can show up when you're constantly multitasking, overworking, or saying yes (i.e., people pleasing).

You may frequently:

- Work well into evenings, weekends, or even during vacations.
- Constantly connect via emails, messages, and work-related calls, even outside regular working hours.
- Have difficulty switching off, even when you're physically away from the office.
- Remain preoccupied with work-related thoughts, leading to mental fatigue. (My husband often does this; I can just tell by the look on his face that he's thinking about work, even if we're out doing something fun, like walking the dog.)
- Lack downtime, which is essential for recharging and preventing burnout.

- Have no time and energy for relationships, hobbies, and self-care.
- Decrease focus and productivity as you constantly shift between work and personal tasks, reducing your ability to concentrate and be productive.

Boundaries are the gift we give ourselves and everyone around us. I dive more into the benefits of boundaries and how to set them in the next chapter on work/life balance.

The "Never-Ending-To-Do" Lister

While lists are great for staying organized, they can also become a trap if we never give ourselves a break. Lists that give everything the same importance and urgency may feel like turning a marathon into a sprint, meaning Listers run out of steam.

You may be prone to:

- Saying yes to everything and anything can lead to a mountain of tasks.
- Striving for perfection.
- Doing it all without delegating.
- Underestimating how much time tasks take.
- Tech overload/being bombarded by notifications.
- Failing to separate work and personal tasks.

I dive more into how to recognize your priorities and create an achievable plan for your day in the time-planning chapter.

The Overachiever

You're hitting all your goals, exceeding expectations, and basically rocking it. But deep down, you're feeling empty, stressed, and like a hamster on a wheel. You feel like you always need another achievement or to obtain something material to feel fulfilled.

Does this sound like you?

- Taking on too many tasks or projects simultaneously
- Setting unrealistically high standards
- Constantly pushing yourself without taking breaks
- Striving for flawlessness in every aspect of work
- Focusing solely on work and ignoring personal well-being
- Feeling reluctant to share responsibilities or delegate tasks

Overachievers are often seen as highly ambitious and successful people, but they can also be prone to burnout.

Burnout isn't just about feeling tired; it's also about feeling emotionally drained, losing your sense of purpose, and often not even realizing it until you're deep in the burnout pit.

So instead of setting an impossible standard for yourself, take small steps toward something more manageable that will still feel like an accomplishment. And when you do reach your goals, take a well-deserved break!

The key is to pay attention to those early warning signs. Are you feeling more irritable? Are you losing interest in things you used to enjoy? Are you neglecting self-care? Did you feel like you met a lot of the traits mentioned above? These are the breadcrumbs leading to burnout, and it's crucial to follow them.

Here are some **general signs** you may want to watch out for:

- Feeling like there's never enough time in the day
- Feeling guilt when you take time for yourself or that you're not working hard enough
- Chronic exhaustion and stress
- Putting other people's needs in front of your own
- Setting unrealistic expectations for yourself (and others) so that no matter what happens, it won't live up to what you wanted it to be

Do you feel like you still struggle to cope and maintain a life that used to seem so effortless? Are you worried you might be pushing yourself to the point of mental, emotional, and physical exhaustion?

Take the free quiz on my website (https://www.bestdlife.com/selfcare-quiz) to find out how close to burnout you may be. You'll also get some simple next steps to help you show up every day as your best, well-cared-for self!

Impact on Health and Well-Being

Now, let's dive into the nitty-gritty of burnout. People talk about the possible mental, physical, and emotional impacts of burnout, but what does that really mean?

Physically, it's not just the occasional tiredness; it's the persistent fatigue or even a zombie-like exhaustion I remember the first week after having a newborn—I could've fallen asleep standing up! You might also experience muscle tension or headaches.

Picture this: You used to handle stress like a champ, but suddenly you're snapping at your favorite people over tiny things, and that's just not who you are. Your emotional resilience takes a nosedive, and you find yourself frequently on the verge of tears over seemingly nothing.

Mentally, it's not just a casual forgetfulness; it's like your thoughts are flying out as quickly as they come (*"Why did I walk in here?"*). Concentration becomes a game of hide-and-seek, and even making simple decisions feels hard.

Now, if we let burnout hang around long enough, chronic insomnia might kick in (*Hello, 2:33 a.m.!*), turning your nights into restless tossing and turning. Emotional consequences might escalate to full-blown anxiety, or, in some cases, depression. And mentally, the fog doesn't just lift on its own—it might linger, affecting your ability to think clearly and solve problems, not to mention the effects it can have on your relationships, work performance, and overall life satisfaction.

So as we wrap up our overview of burnout, I want to step into the realm of work/life balance. But hey, it's not just talk. I've developed some serious strategies to prevent burnout and ways to bounce back when it sneaks up on you. So stick around, because we're in this together, and there's a lot more to unfold in this journey toward happiness, balance, and overall well-being.

Chapter 2
Finding Your Work-Life Balance

"Work-life balance is not an entitlement or benefit. Your company cannot give it to you. You have to create it for yourself."

— Matthew Kelly

It's hard to find that elusive life balance, isn't it?

Now, I know some of you may not like the word "balance." You might even be thinking, "There's no way for everything to be equal!" (You're not wrong.)

You might prefer to call it "work/life flow" or "work/life harmony." I get it, but in this book, I'm using the word "balance" and redefining how we use it and what it means.

The "Perfect Balance" Myth

First things first: I want to bust the "perfect balance" myth. The idea that we can perfectly divide our time and energy among all aspects of everyday life is not realistic, so holding yourself to that kind of standard sets you up for failure. Let's stop chasing this mythical balance and embrace life's messiness.

So what *does* balance mean, then?

At its core, work-life balance is all about finding a healthy relationship between your work life and your personal life. And this can look different depending on the day. It's about making sure that your job doesn't take over every aspect of your life, and that you can enjoy personal time outside of work without feeling guilty, overwhelmed, or burned out.

It's so important to recognize that achieving a work-life balance is a journey, not a destination. It can change throughout the year or different seasons of your life. It's something that requires constant effort and attention (i.e., *practice*), and there's no one-size-fits-all solution.

Now, don't think, "Ugh, too much work. I'm out," because with some strategic steps, not only is it possible and manageable, but it's *so* worth it!

Why Is Work-Life Balance Important?

Well, for starters, a work-life balance is crucial for our mental and physical health. Constant work and stress can lead to anxiety, burnout, and even physical health problems like heart disease and high blood pressure. Also, having a healthy balance between work and personal life can lead to greater overall life satisfaction, happiness, and fulfillment.

But here's the thing: Achieving work-life balance doesn't mean completely disconnecting from work and living on a beach somewhere (although that does sound pretty nice, doesn't it?).

It's about finding a rhythm between the different facets of your life that work for you and your unique situation. It's about recognizing that there will be times when your job/business will demand more of your time and energy, and other times when you need to prioritize your personal life.

Ensuring you set aside time for fun activities and self-care will help you become better equipped to navigate those unexpected "life" moments, both at work and in your personal life.

Moreover, maintaining a balance encourages positive relationships with family, friends, or significant others. That quality helps build a sense of trust and prevents the strain that can result from neglecting these relationships.

In terms of professional benefits, achieving a work-life balance enhances productivity and efficiency. Taking regular breaks and having time away from work leads to improved focus and creativity when returning to professional tasks.

Creating balance between work and personal life also improves your personal growth and development. Pursuing hobbies, interests, and self-care activities outside of work contributes to a more well-rounded, fulfilling and enriched life, positively influencing both your personal and professional development.

Ultimately, a work-life balance is about creating a sustainable life in your career and your personal relationships. It's about finding ways to incorporate the things you love into your daily routine, while also ensuring that you have the time and energy to be present in your relationships and other activities outside of work.

Lisa was known for her ability to juggle multiple projects and always meet deadlines. Her colleagues admired her work ethic, and her boss often relied on her to take on the most challenging tasks. From the outside, it seemed like Lisa had it all together—she was successful at work, had a loving family, and was known for being dependable.

But behind the scenes, Lisa's life was far from balanced. Her workdays started early and ended late, often bleeding into her weekends. She found herself constantly checking emails at the dinner table, taking calls during her kids' soccer games, and even pulling out her laptop to work before bed. The lines between her professional and personal life were so blurred that she couldn't remember the last time she truly relaxed.

When Lisa came to me, she was desperate to regain control over her life. We started by assessing her current routine and identifying the areas where work was encroaching on her personal time. Lisa admitted that she found it hard to say no to extra work, fearing it might make her seem less dedicated or reliable.

We worked together to set clear boundaries between her work and personal life. Lisa began scheduling "unplugged" time, where she would disconnect from work entirely, dedicating that time to her family and herself. She also started prioritizing her tasks more effectively, delegating when possible and learning to say no to nonessential projects.

Lisa worried that setting boundaries might disappoint her boss or colleagues. But as she stuck with the new routine, she noticed something surprising—her productivity at work actually improved. By giving herself time to recharge, she found she could focus better and complete tasks more efficiently.

Outside of work, Lisa began to reconnect with her family and rediscover hobbies she had long abandoned. She started going for more walks, reading, and even returned to painting, something she hadn't done in years. Over time, Lisa's work/life balance improved dramatically. She was still dedicated to her job, but it no longer consumed her entire life.

What Is Balance?

When you're looking for balance, the biggest thing to remember is that it comes from within.

Balanced people tend to feel more motivated and less stressed and can increase their overall productivity at work, at home, and in life. And yet, so often, we allow ourselves to walk around, feeling off-balance for days.

For example, you might worry about things you have no control over or feel blocked with self-doubt, negative thoughts, or limiting beliefs. All of those mental mind games can put you in an unbalanced state and keep you from taking action.

Instead, imagine you feel comfortable, accepting, open, honest, and confident. You're prepared for what life throws at you and can react calmly and assertively to negative events. If life kicks you in the head, you can avoid the conflict with a graceful sidestep and a wise smile.

A couple years ago, I practiced balance as I taught my daughter how to drive. As she took a much-too-fast turn into oncoming traffic, I (of course) gritted my teeth and wished I had an emergency brake pedal on my side of the car.

My past self might have dramatically grabbed the steering wheel, let out a scream, and lambasted her about how scary-bad the turn was, only increasing her anxiety and frustration.

I took a deep breath, slowly let it out, smiled, and calmly let her know she was doing great, but that she "may want to slow down a little" on the turns thereafter.

She matched my leveled response with a jaunty, "Okay, Mom!" and adjusted her next turn attempt. I felt good that I didn't overreact and make the rest of the ride miserable for both of us.

It's a simple concept, but sadly, most of us walk around feeling off-balance and accepting it as "the norm." But getting into balance isn't difficult in and of itself. It's difficult because most don't recognize the internal struggle putting them off-balance in the first place.

Instead of everything being equal, I believe balance means our ability to:

- Adapt
- Pivot
- Show resilience
- Set boundaries

Adapting

Adapting allows you to change your ideas or behavior to successfully deal with the unexpected chaos of life. Sometimes called "emotional agility," it means you feel confident that you can find *a* solution, rather than resort to the *only* solution you've ever relied on. You can see opportunities, use positive self-talk, maintain flexibility, and break habits as situations warrant. In short, you can zig and zag easily and confidently.

Pivoting

Pivoting is essentially about flexibility to see all the options. It's like having a plan but being open to adjustments when life throws curveballs.

Picture this: You've got your work tasks neatly lined up, and suddenly, you get a call that your kid has vomited and has to be picked up from school ASAP. Instead of stressing out, you rearrange your schedule, maybe delegate some tasks, and ensure both work and personal life get the attention they deserve.

Showing Resilience

Showing resilience is your ability to bounce back, in your own way, no matter how difficult things may seem. Life can stretch you, force you to cope in new or challenging situations, but then you can return to "normal."

Resilience isn't just about working hard. It also requires you to stop, rest, and recover. Recovery is not only the key to maintaining good health but also preventing lost productivity. To build resilience, you need to be willing to stop and take care of yourself. This can mean spending some time away from your phone, eating lunch away from your desk, and actually using your vacation time.

Setting Boundaries

Setting boundaries is, I believe, the most important of the four abilities, and "boundaries" is my favorite B-word. Now, when I say that word, what do you think of? Walls? Something negative? Saying "no" to tasks? Removing things?

I want to help you see that boundaries mean so much more than that. Boundaries can *add* things, like space in your day, freedom from guilt and mental fatigue, and can infuse more fun and joy into your life. Let's dive a little deeper.

The Power of Boundaries

We were taught as kids to be kind, likable, and helpful in order to please others—but at what cost?

Kevin was a dedicated worker. From the beginning of his career, he believed that being available around the clock was the key to success. This mindset was reinforced early on when a senior manager praised him for taking a client call late at night, saying, "This is what it takes to get ahead."

Kevin took that to heart and made it his mission to be the most reliable person on his team. Over the years, this drive to always be available became part of Kevin's identity. He was the guy who never said no, who always made time for last-minute requests, and who could be counted on in a pinch. His clients loved him, his boss relied on him, and his colleagues admired his work ethic. But as Kevin's responsibilities grew, so did the demands on his time.

Before long, Kevin's workdays began earlier and ended later. He was answering emails at all hours, taking calls during family dinners, and even working on weekends. His personal life started to suffer—he missed his kids' school events, rarely saw his friends, and hadn't taken a real vacation in years. But Kevin didn't think he could afford to set boundaries. After all, wasn't this what it took to be successful?

The turning point came during his daughter's birthday party. As Kevin found himself checking emails instead of enjoying the celebration, he realized just how disconnected he had become. The stress of always being "on" was also starting to affect his health—he wasn't sleeping well, he felt constantly exhausted, and his patience was wearing thin. That's when he knew something had to change.

Kevin struggled in setting boundaries. He was afraid that saying no or stepping back would make him seem less committed. We started by exploring where this fear came from. Kevin realized that his need to be constantly available stemmed from a deep-seated fear of disappointing others or being seen as replaceable.

Together, we worked on small, manageable steps to help Kevin start setting boundaries. He began by establishing "off hours" when he wouldn't check emails or take work calls. Kevin also practiced communicating his boundaries clearly and confidently. He started informing clients when he was available and delegating tasks to his team during off-hours. Over time, he noticed that not only did his clients adjust, but they also appreciated the clarity and structure. Kevin's relationships at work improved as he was no longer stretched so thin, and he had more energy and focus during his working hours.

In the end, Kevin's journey taught him that the relentless pursuit of being indispensable had come at a cost, and that true success included taking care of himself. By understanding where his struggle with boundaries originated and working to change his habits, Kevin found a way to excel in his career while also enjoying a balanced and fulfilling personal life.

Without boundaries, we run the risk of being taken advantage of, and ultimately giving up power over our lives.

Someone once told me, "Your time and energy are like a precious currency—more precious than gold. Once it's spent, it's gone."

It's true.

Implementing boundaries in your own life is no different than setting a bedtime for your kids. You're setting healthy limits for how people treat you and what you will (and will not) tolerate when working together.

Boundaries can help you determine what does and does not get your attention so you can focus on what's most important, be more productive, and actually achieve your goals. This can be as simple as putting your phone on silent when you eat dinner with your family or refusing to work on weekends.

Establish guidelines, rules, or limits so you can identify the behaviors you will accept from others, what you will not, and how much you will take on before you will confidently say, "No."

Boundaries can offer predictability and a sense of security so you're not always reacting or on the defensive.

How Workplace Policies Affect Work/Life Balance

Workplace policies can set the tone for how employees navigate their professional and personal rhythms. The culture and policies can dictate how you structure your day and take care of yourself, as well as how much your job/business works *with* your life, rather than against it.

Just as you have certain things you look for in a partner (trustworthiness, honesty, sense of humor) or when buying a home (three bedrooms, two baths, garage), you may consider specific criteria in your professional life to help you achieve a better work/ life balance:

- **Flexible hours:** Flexible hours allow you to adjust your work time to sync with your peak productivity periods or to accommodate personal commitments. A Future Forum Pulse survey revealed that employees with flexible schedules experience a 39% higher productivity rate than employees without flexibility.
- **Remote work options:** Whether you opt for a home office, a co-working space, or a coffee shop, remote work can empower you to find a productive groove. I enjoy rotating to a couple of different spots. I find that each location energizes me differently. Studies show that employees with remote work options can achieve better health, less stress, higher productivity levels, decreased turnover, and reduced absenteeism.
- **Vacation and leave policies:** Adequate vacation and leave allowances gives employees the chance to recharge and come back to work with renewed energy. In a 2023 study by the Pew Research Center, less than half of U.S. workers (about 46%) who receive paid leave time take it. When asked why, employees say they don't feel they need to take more, or worry about falling behind at work, or feel

bad about their co-workers taking on additional work. A higher percentage of women than men report feeling this way.

- **Clear expectations:** Employees who know what's expected of them and have a clear understanding of their job expectations (without hidden meanings or agendas) can achieve a better work/life balance.
- **Supportive culture:** This one's *key*! When colleagues and leadership encourage a healthy balance, it creates a supportive environment where employees feel comfortable taking breaks and prioritizing self-care. Studies show that having a culture of wellness fosters stronger team collaboration and communication. When employees feel supported and valued, they are more likely to collaborate, share ideas, and work together effectively.

Now, I recognize not all of these are possible depending on the field you work in.

For example, my job in education doesn't allow for flexible hours or remote work options—I have to be there when the students are there. But I also know that having a set schedule helped with my boundaries. I enjoyed and needed the friendships and support of my colleagues.

My husband's job, however, allows both remote and in-office hours. While my options are different, that doesn't mean I wasn't able to create my own work/life balance; I just learned how to set it up in a way that worked best for me.

The Role of Stress in Work-Life Balance

It's safe to say that burnout involves stress. People often talk about stress and burnout together (and sometimes they use the words interchangeably), but there are differences between the two.

Here's how I describe the biggest difference: Imagine you have a bonfire. The more wood you add (tasks on your to-do list), the bigger the fire gets (your feelings of stress). You can continue to add more wood and create a bigger fire for periods of time.

Now, burnout is most like the smoking ashes and embers left after the fire burns down. You can try throwing more wood on it to rebuild the fire, but you only get a few small glows from the embers and more smoke because the fire (your energy) is all burned out. The goal of creating work/life balance is to manage the amount of wood (tasks) you put on the fire so that it stays at a manageable flame (workable amount of stress).

In the workplace, stress can cost companies millions of dollars a year, through increased absenteeism and detachment, as well as decreased productivity and employee retention. Stress can come from intense pressure from the demands of the job, long hours, strained relations with co-workers or supervisors, and/or an overall lack of work-life balance.

Stress at home can affect your relationships, disrupt your sleep, and take a toll on your overall well-being. Stress-relief programs and activities have been proven to increase focus, creativity, resilience, and collaboration, and reduce stress and distractedness at home and work.

The Power of Habits

Living a lifestyle you love has nothing to do with wanting, wishing, willing, or dreaming it into existence.

It comes from *doing*. The things you do every day help imprint and automate behaviors and ensure that they happen consistently. These things are better known as *habits*. Habits are repeated behaviors that can either propel us forward or hold us back. By intentionally cultivating positive habits, we can construct a framework that aligns with our goals, ultimately influencing our long-term success.

Benefits of Habits

Habits make up about 40% of what you do every day. It doesn't matter if they're good or bad—if done consistently, they provide the pulse for your day.

By examining the habits you currently have, as well as those you want to add, you can make the choice to "habit" yourself into the life you want to lead. Habits help you feel less stressed, help you use your time more productively, and make your day run more smoothly.

The idea of adding habits and systems can sound overwhelming. You may be thinking, " *I'm already stretched so thin—how could I possibly add one more thing?"*

Here's the deal: Habits actually *give* you more time and free up space to do the things you want to do (even if it's doing nothing at all).

The right habits and strategies can help you:

- Become unstuck from a draining or unfulfilling routine.
- Carve out more time to do the things you love with the people you care about.
- Find a consistent, efficient flow and calm in your day-to-day life.
- Release self-doubt or limiting beliefs around opportunities you want to explore.

Habits play a huge role in creating work/life balance. Habits help ensure the things you want to happen consistently actually do. Automating the actions in your life that happen daily will reduce stress and decision fatigue, and can even help you to add new habits to your day through habit stacking.

Together, habits and automation form a powerful duo, helping you to navigate the complexities of modern life with a balanced and intentional approach. Whether it's the rituals we consciously and consistently instill or the automated systems we implement, these elements play a pivotal role in shaping our daily experiences and contributing to sustained well-being.

Create a brief list of some habits you want to start working on.

_____

_____

_____

Decision Fatigue

I don't know about you, but I notice that I have more trouble making decisions or sticking with a new (good!) habit at the end of each day. I often feel too rushed to figure out what to have for dinner or too tired to fit in a workout.

Decision fatigue happens because we all have a finite amount of energy that we can put into making decisions in any given day. They say that's why Steve Jobs always wore a black turtleneck and jeans—he gave himself one less thing to think about every morning.

By automating certain areas of our lives, we can save our energy for the things that really need it. Having both a morning and afternoon routine can help reduce decision fatigue, and also ensure that you incorporate self-care consistently into your day. It also frees brain space for more creative and productive thinking.

Maybe you already have a morning routine. You get up, pour a mug of steaming coffee, read the paper or check email, and fix some toast before heading into the shower.

Or do you wrap up your day with a bedtime routine? A bedtime routine not only helps you out when you're too tired to make smart choices, but it also guides you toward falling asleep more easily.

Sit down and think about the parts of your day and week you can turn into routines. Write them down and create daily to-do lists for yourself until you've established these new habits and routines. Spending a little bit of time creating routines and habits will make your days run a lot smoother, because fewer decisions equals less fatigue.

AM Habits _____

_____

_____

PM Habits _____

_____

_____

You might find yourself less stressed and get more done during your productive hours, and that's a beautiful thing.

Another way to gain the benefits is to add these new things to a habit you already have, which is called habit stacking, an amazing concept outlined by James Clear in the book *Atomic Habits*.

For example, you've already integrated the habit of brushing your teeth into your day. Use that opportunity to add at least three to five minutes of whatever you otherwise can't find time for, whether it's meditating, doing some squats, planning your day, doing nothing, putting on your favorite song, doing a little dance, smelling your favorite lotion, or just taking time to breathe.

It can help you find confidence, peace, empowerment, or anything else they're looking for. These areas all help contribute to your mental fitness.

Incorporate a system to ensure you consciously integrate routines and practices to build your physical strength and mental resilience. It'll change your life! I promise.

Role of Technology

Technology plays a dual role when it comes to work/life balance. Not only is it part of the problem, but it's also part of the solution.

As part of the problem, think about those constant notifications and email pings: They give you the expectation that you're always supposed to be "on" and available, don't they? Your inbox rules you with its never-ending to-do list; your phone is the taskmaster. You finish one task, and then *bam*, another one pops up.

This digital whirlwind can drown you in a sea of unread messages. Social media can increase pressure with its expectations to measure up to the seemingly "perfect lives" everyone else posts.

Now, the tech perks! Tools and apps can help streamline repetitive tasks and provide organization and reminders to decrease your mental load and fatigue. It can automate tasks, streamline processes, and make workdays less of a circus.

But here's the catch: Finding the right balance is like walking a tightrope. Too much tech, and you risk burning out from information overload. Too little, and you might miss out on efficiency gains. So, use technology to enhance your life, not complicate it.

As we wrap up striking that delicate balance between work and life, it's time to pivot. In the chapters ahead, we'll dive into strategies that will help you transform feeling overwhelmed, exhausted, and burned out into empowerment, efficiency, and happiness. Let's embark on this path together, where empowerment becomes the light, guiding you through your next steps.

Chapter 3
Building Mental Fitness

"We are stronger, gentler, more resilient, and more beautiful than any of us imagine."

– Mark Nepo

What is Mental Fitness?

Most people have a clear idea of what "physical fitness" means. They can tell you what they think it looks like and what they would have to do to get physically fit (eat right, exercise, etc.).

So what do you think of when I use the phrase "mental fitness?"

Not sure how to answer that?

Mental fitness forms the foundation for your mental and emotional resilience. It can also help you handle the ups and downs life throws at you. In other words, mental fitness creates a state of well-being that keeps your brain and emotional health in check, and includes many habits, routines, structure, consistency, and practices to help you proactively and preventatively maintain your overall health.

Some people assume mental fitness is just a trait you either have or don't have, but you can train and strengthen it, much like physical fitness.

Let's start reframing how you think about mental wellness and health, so you can think of mental fitness the same way you think about physical fitness.

As you know, even though you are physically fit you can still experience some minor pulls, strains, and areas of weakness. Just like physical fitness, having strong mental fitness doesn't entirely protect you from occasionally getting hurt from life experiences.

Mental fitness is a foundation to help you adapt, pivot, set boundaries, and be resilient—the things you need to find balance every day. As you develop the skills we talk about later in the book through the Exhausted to Empowered Formula, you'll also build your mental fitness. You'll practice these skills so you reach a point where you do them automatically, without thinking about it.

Automating those skills helps you better handle all the unexpected moments life brings you. Integrating them as part of your daily routine helps make them an easy part of your lifestyle.

Why it Matters

You typically don't do anything once and expect results: You don't eat once. You don't breathe once. You don't shower once. You don't work out once because doing it just once won't give you long-term results.

So why would you expect anything different with your habits or self-care routine when you're trying to find work/life balance?

Have you ever said this?

"Oh yeah—I tried that once and it didn't work."

Unfortunately, trying out a new routine once doesn't cut it. It takes one small step one day, another small step the next… and the next. While that can seem so simple to understand, it can be so hard to *do*. Success results in small actions taken over time. Success is the difference between wanting to do XYZ (insert that "thing" you keep saying you'll do when you have more time) and actually *achieving* XYZ.

The people who achieve their goals know it's not about just thinking, wishing, or trying something once. It's about changing not just what they do daily, but also how they *think* every day.

Your mental fitness routine helps you:

- Keep going on the days you don't feel like it
- Build resilience to cope with stress
- Take care of yourself every day

What's at Risk?

Neglecting to develop and maintain your mental fitness can pose several risks and challenges to your overall well-being and quality of life:

- **Decreased cognitive function:** Without mental stimulation and cognitive challenges, your brain's cognitive functions may decline over time. This can manifest as difficulties with memory, attention, concentration, problem solving, and decision-making, impacting your ability to perform daily tasks effectively.
- **Increased stress and anxiety:** Without effective stress management strategies and emotional regulation skills, you may experience chronic stress, burnout, and negative effects on your physical health.
- **Impaired emotional well-being:** Neglecting mental fitness can lead to emotional dysregulation, mood swings, and difficulties managing emotions. Impaired well-being can result in heightened emotional reactivity, irritability, mood disorders such as depression or anxiety disorders, and challenges in interpersonal relationships.
- **Reduced resilience:** Mental fitness builds resilience and coping skills to navigate life's challenges and setbacks. Without resilience, you may struggle to bounce back from adversity, cope with stressors, and effectively adapt to changes.
- **Decline in overall well-being:** Not building mental fitness can lead to feelings of dissatisfaction, low self-esteem, lack of motivation, social withdrawal, and a diminished sense of purpose and fulfillment.

- **Increased risk of mental health disorders:** Neglecting mental fitness can contribute to mental health disorders such as depression, anxiety disorders, bipolar disorder, post-traumatic stress disorder (PTSD), substance abuse disorders, and other psychiatric conditions.
- **Impact on physical health:** Neglecting mental well-being can have adverse effects on physical health outcomes. Chronic stress, anxiety, and mood disorders can contribute to cardiovascular problems, weakened immune function, digestive issues, sleep disturbances, and other health complications.
- **Impaired relationships and social connections:** Poor mental fitness can strain relationships, lead to social isolation, and hinder your ability to connect with others empathetically. It may result in communication challenges, conflicts, and difficulties forming and maintaining meaningful relationships.

You can prioritize mental fitness through proactive self-care practices, stress management techniques, mindfulness, cognitive stimulation, and seeking support when needed. But how, exactly?

Let's find out.

Ways to Start Building Your Mental Fitness

Just as you would start a physical fitness routine, we will incorporate some of the same training techniques for your mental fitness.

First, decide which areas you want to work on so you know which exercises and mental muscles you need to strengthen.

Choose the Easy Option

We don't avoid easy things as much as we avoid hard things, so the next step is to keep it simple and easy. Finding success doesn't always have to come from doing hard things. It's also easier to remember to do the "easy" stuff.

Sometimes, the easy thing is also more successful than something more time-consuming and complicated. For example, people *always* rave about my go-to artichoke spinach dip and ask for the recipe, and it's honestly so simple to whip up. If you want to try it yourself, I've included the recipe in the back of the book—you're welcome!

Do you struggle to see all options available to you? Do you find yourself saying "yes" to everything? Or maybe you get stuck in a perfection-procrastination loop?

Recognize that there's no one way to work on your mental fitness. You'll want some diversity to keep you from being bored. When things are boring, you become less engaged and committed, which, unfortunately, stops you from doing them.

We are not one-dimensional, so we need to approach things in a multifaceted way to help us strengthen various areas. It helps us cope in different ways, pivot, adapt, have a different perspective, see things differently, and incorporate different strategies to achieve an overall mental fitness goal.

Ultimately, doing things consistently and in a way that feels effortless is how we find success that offers ease and breathing room.

Developing mental fitness involves practicing activities that enhance cognitive function, emotional resilience, and overall well-being. I cover these more in depth in the self-care chapter with action steps.

Third, be consistent by practicing every day. Practicing while you're relaxed helps create muscle memory to connect your actions to feeling relaxed. You'll integrate it as part of your day-to-day life. Since it's something you already do regularly, you'll continue to do it even if you feel slightly stressed.

You get the benefits of consistency by building onto the self-care habits you already have. For example, the other day, someone said to me how she doesn't think brushing her teeth is self-care. I told her I agree that brushing your teeth in and of itself might not be self-care, but it's an easy opportunity to add another self-care step (called Habit Stacking by James Clear in his book Atomic Habits).

Since you've already integrated brushing your teeth into your day, use that opportunity to add at least two to three minutes of whatever you otherwise can't find time for, whether it's journaling, doing some squats, putting on your favorite song, doing a little dance, smelling your favorite lotion, or just taking a moment to breathe and practice positive thoughts or gratitude.

Adding these new things to a habit you already have is called habit stacking, so it becomes a routine and creates consistency. Depending on your goal, you can build a system around it.

I incorporate habit stacking with the clients I work with. Depending on what they're working on, whether improving their sleep, the way they think about money, their organization, their sense of style, etc., we find opportunities throughout the day where they can habit stack to accomplish their goals. It ultimately helps them consistently find confidence, peace, empowerment, and more.

And these steps are all connected. For example, if you're stressed about money, you won't be mentally in a good place to relax. If you're not relaxed or getting a good night's sleep, you'll be tired. If you're fatigued, you'll be irritable and maybe fall into old habits of not eating well and not moving your body, the list goes on. All these things will impact your mental fitness.

Are you ready to create a system to consciously integrate routines and practices to strengthen yourself for resilient mental and physical fitness? Awesome - then let's dive in!

Part 2

The Exhausted to Empowered Formula

If you want to actually feel like you've "got it together" and know exactly what needs to happen in your life, you must have a plan and include time for fun or relaxation every day, then you're in the right place!.

The Exhausted to Empowered Formula is my signature framework to guide you to let go of overwhelming and guilty feelings and enjoy your life.

The principles themselves are simple. They sound like common sense, which is why we might not give them the attention they need to be effective. However, they still take work so you feel the benefits.

I love talking about the Exhausted to Empowered Formula, and I can't wait to share it with you!

The Three Pillars

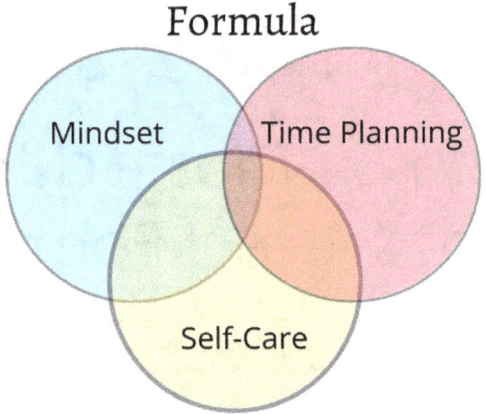

The Exhausted to Empowered Formula contains three pillars, which work together to help create calm and ease in your day: Mindset, Time Planning, and Self-Care. We'll look at them in more detail in the following chapters.

While I've inserted many checklists in this section, they are there for you to see and get an idea of what each pillar entails, but please don't feel pressured to do them all now. You'll have access to all the self-assessment pieces and action steps in your free workbook You can access the workbook here - https://subscribepage.io/balance-breakthrough, but for now, let's walk through each pillar.

Mindset

Mindset is the cornerstone that determines how you perceive and approach your daily events and responsibilities. Cultivating a positive and resilient mindset can reshape your experience, turning challenges into opportunities for better outcomes. We will talk about what mindset is and how it differs from mindfulness, the difference between a fixed and a growth mindset, how to change your mindset, the role limiting beliefs play in this process, and how mindset affects the way you view and use your time.

Time Planning

Time planning is more than a practical tool to ensure efficiency and effectiveness in your daily endeavors. By mastering the art of prioritization and organization, you'll discover a newfound control over your schedule, minimizing feeling overwhelmed. Time planning involves breaking down your day by analyzing how you currently spend your time, and prioritizing where your time goes. We'll look at things that can get in the way, like procrastination, saying no, and strategies for seamlessly integrating work, life, and self-care.

Self-Care

Lastly, many people overlook self-care. Integrating self-care practices into your routine fosters rejuvenation and enhances your capacity to meet demands with vitality. I'll define and potentially reframe what you think of as self-care, break down the eight categories that make up a practical self-care practice, and outline steps to start building your own practice, which is a fundamental part of preventing burnout.

Together, these three pillars create a robust foundation to empower you to navigate the demands of life with intention, balance, and resilience. As we delve into each pillar, we'll unravel practical insights and actionable strategies to uncover a transformative journey toward a harmonious and fulfilling life.

Chapter 4

The Power of Mindset

"Everything begins from the mind, including change. So, if you want to alter your life, you have to start with your mindset."

— Alexi Weaver

I believe when you think differently, you feel differently, and when you feel differently, you act differently. So, when working with clients who want to make a change, we begin with mindset, the first step in my Exhausted to Empowered Formula.

Often, I see people dive in and start with the action they want to take, such as going to the gym, launching into a diet, decluttering their closets, etc., without working through the thoughts and feelings that got them there in the first place.

Without working through and understanding your existing patterns and beliefs, you can end up falling back into old habits.

What Is Mindset?

Mindset is a series of self-perceptions or beliefs people hold about themselves. These determine behavior, outlook, and mental attitude. For example, believing you are either *capable* or *incapable* of doing something is a mindset.

It's no secret that our mindset plays a major role in our lives. It controls our thoughts, our feelings, and how we view the world. The person we talk to most in the entire world is ourselves, and so our thoughts (based on our mindset) are the internal monologue that narrates every aspect of our lives, impacting how we feel.

Ultimately, it's safe to say that our mindset forms the roadmap to every detail of our lives. It directs and channels our thoughts, actions, and emotions, and plays a critical role in how we think about life events.

To achieve your goals and the lifestyle you want, your mindset needs to match your desires and values. Otherwise, it might hold you back from getting where you want to be.

Mindset vs. Mindfulness

I often hear the words "mindset" and "mindfulness" used interchangeably, but they're actually different.

Mindfulness is about being present with your surroundings in the moment. Paying attention to your senses is typically a part of this practice. It's a very effective part of self-care, so I'll cover more of the specifics in a later chapter.

Mindset is the perspective you take and the way you think about the events that happen in your life. Your mindset determines whether you view a situation as positive or negative, possible or impossible, and yourself as capable or incapable.

Fixed vs. Growth Mindset

There are two main types of mindset: a fixed mindset and a growth mindset.

A fixed mindset assumes that our abilities, intelligence, and life situation are set in stone, and that we can't change in any way. People with a fixed mindset believe they're "stuck" and do not have the ability to change or do better for themselves. When you have a rigid or fixed mindset, you might allow your passion (your kids, a relationship, or your job/business) to become your whole world. This can lead to self-doubt and guilt if you take a break. You spend your time focused on what you think you "should do" versus having the flexibility to take breaks and spend time on other interests.

A person with a growth mindset believes in potential and possibility. They believe they have the skills and abilities to improve their situation. These individuals see failure as a springboard for learning and improving, not the end of the road. This can be as simple as adding the word "yet" to the end of your sentence, like: "I don't know how to ski yet" or "I'm not good at math yet." They know that with time, grace, practice, and skill-building, the situation can improve.

Having a growth mindset will help you:

- broaden your beliefs about what it means to be a good employee, partner, mom, etc.
- reframe how you prioritize your time and yourself,
- redefine what "counts" as self-care,
- undo the limiting beliefs or guilt that can hold you back from taking time for yourself and being truly present in each moment.

Do you have a fixed mindset or a growth mindset? Not sure?

Here's a quick checklist to help you gauge whether you lean more toward a fixed or a growth mindset:

Fixed mindset:

- I avoid challenges because I'm afraid of failure.
- When I face setbacks, I often give up easily.
- Constructive criticism feels like a personal attack.
- I believe my abilities and intelligence are fixed traits.
- Others' success makes me feel threatened or envious.
- I stick to what I know and rarely venture outside my comfort zone.

Growth mindset:

- I see challenges as opportunities to learn and grow.
- Setbacks motivate me to work harder and try different strategies.
- I view constructive criticism as valuable feedback for improvement.
- I believe that I can develop my abilities and intelligence over time.
- Others' success inspires and motivates me.
- I actively seek out new experiences and challenges to expand my skills.

Reflect on these statements, and if you find yourself leaning more toward a growth mindset, great! If not, don't worry. Awareness is the first step, and you can work on developing a growth mindset over time.

In the next section, let's look at strategies that will help you start doing just that!

Changing Your Mindset

Luckily, your mindset is something that you have the power to change. Why should you?

Because your Thoughts → Feelings → Actions.

If you want a successful life, you have to start with your thoughts. If you start with the action without changing your thoughts, you won't have the investment in the positive effect or impact you're looking for.

Grab a piece of paper or open your Notes app (or bookmark this for later) and do the following exercise.

Recognize Your Thoughts

It's hard to change your mindset if you don't acknowledge your thoughts. This isn't about judging or agreeing with them—just recognize them and how they make you feel. A great way to do this is to write them down—both positive and negative (or speak them into a document to make it easy to express them).

Growing up, I would say I was a dancer, a student, a daughter, but I wouldn't have used the word "athlete" to describe myself.

I believed an athlete was someone who was fast, incredibly skilled, and always picked first for the team. While I played some sports (soccer, tennis, lacrosse, dance), I was never what I would call "the best." As I got older, I kept joining teams, but just for fun.

In my early thirties, I began running. I competed in many local races, and over the span of many years, amassed a collection of race bibs and participation medals.

I didn't win once, but as I ran, I hung out with other runners. I began to shift my mindset and call myself an athlete. It became more about the act of being a regular participant rather than about winning. I realized I was winning just by showing up and being a part of the activity, regardless of my ability. This mental pivot into possibility and ability to learn a new skill is what it looks like to have a growth mindset.

Write down three to five negative thoughts you've had in the past:

_____

_____

_____

_____

Separate Yourself from Your Thoughts

Unfortunately, many of the things we say to ourselves are harsh and typically not true. (We'll talk about this in the next section on limiting beliefs.) It can be easy to give in to our thoughts of guilt, shame, blame, or our beliefs of other people's expectations or judgments. We can see more options and possibilities when we are not clouded by our own internal negative monologue.

Where Are You Focusing?

For whatever reason, many of us seem programmed to focus on the negative. Instead of paying attention to negative thoughts, we should focus more on positive thoughts.

Two wolves exist inside of us, according to a Native American folktale: a negative, mean wolf and a good, positive wolf. According to the folktale, the negative wolf fights the positive wolf all the time.

But which wolf wins?

The Native Americans say, "The one that you feed."

Take a look at the thoughts you wrote down. Look at the negative thoughts. Are they true? Would you talk about a friend like that? If not, write what you would say and how you would support and speak to someone else.

Notice Outside Influences

They say we become most like the five people we spend the majority of our time with. These people contribute to how we perceive and react to events. When we were younger, we probably spent the most time with our family members, who pass on generational beliefs, either purposefully or not. As we get older, friends and co-workers can influence our mindset. So while our mindset comes from our own thoughts, we need to become intentionally aware of the factors around us that can influence that.

Write down who you spend the majority of your time with:

_____

_____

_____

_____

What are their mindsets? Do they always see themselves as the victim of their circumstances?

People who have a negative spin on everything can rub off on you. The saying, "You are who you hang around" is so true!

Limiting Beliefs

We can't have a conversation about mindset without talking about limiting beliefs. Limiting beliefs are the enemy of a healthy mindset and often rear their ugly heads when you're trying to do something new or make a positive change in your life.

Limiting beliefs (or what I like to call "the mean girl in my head") tell us we "can't" do something, or "should" do something else, or make assumptions about what others are thinking about us. In general, they make us feel bad, insecure, guilty, or fearful when we try to take action.

Those default statements you tell yourself that prevent you from...

- Taking risks
- Trying new things because of a fear of failure
- Doing what's good for you
- Connecting with others

We all have limiting beliefs! Look at the list below and see how many you may have heard or said to yourself:

- I'm not good enough.
- I'm not smart enough.
- I make bad decisions.
- I'm not a good mom, partner, or worker.

- I'm too old to try.
- Taking care of myself means I'm selfish.
- I'm not smart/disciplined/skilled enough.
- If I say no to people, they'll hate me and I'll miss opportunities.

So, how do you stop the negativity and reframe your thoughts so you can get to where you want to be?

Question the Limiting Belief

First, write the thought down. Call it out. Make it known to yourself. Does what you think influence your choices? Does guilt influence your choices? Are you constantly worried about letting others down?

Ask yourself, "Would I say this to a friend?"

Typically the answer is a resounding "No!"

Look at where this belief came from in your life. Your family? Society? Challenge yourself to call it out as incorrect and spend time understanding why. Focus on the "why": Why do you want to do the thing that you have a limiting belief toward?

Ask yourself, "How is this belief serving me?"

Many times, you focus on the what ("I want to lose ten pounds!") and the how ("I need to be better about my diet!"), but completely forget about why.

Knowing your why will continually anchor you when things start to become difficult, keep you motivated, and help you push through any mental blocks or resistance walls that pop up along the way. Because once you know why you're doing something, it puts things in perspective.

We make the time and the effort for the things we want, especially when we focus on why they are important to us.

Some questions to ask yourself to figure out your big "why":

- *What makes this goal important to me?*
- *What will the positive outcomes be if I achieve this?*
- *What will happen if I don't?*
- *Why is now the time?*

Own your "why!"

Create Alternative Beliefs: Positive Affirmations

Next, let's rewrite the narrative with a positive thought to support your actions. Affirmations are a powerful tool to train your mind to focus on the positive and where you want to go, instead of where you are or where you've been.

Now, this doesn't instantly stop the negative thought. It takes time and practice to retrain your brain to go to this new thought.

You create new neural pathways in your brain (sounds pretty scienc-y, right?) But what does this mean?

I like to think of it like going on a hike. The path that gets used the most is worn down and easy to follow. When you try to go in a different direction and create a new path, it takes time and repetition to get it as worn down and easy to follow as the one that's been there for years.

With repeated practice noticing your limiting beliefs and imagining new ideas to replace them, you'll start to notice the thousands of tiny decisions you make based on your limiting beliefs without even realizing it. You'll start to notice that the same limiting beliefs that keep you from looking for a new job are the ones that keep you from wearing the clothes you want to wear—and you'll see how ridiculous it is. And that's when you'll have more control over what you choose to believe.

Practice Your Beliefs and Affirmations: Act as if They Are Already True

Instead of waiting for a specific time or criteria or for something to be true, take the actions now and live as if you've achieved that goal. This might mean taking scary, imperfect action, but do it anyway. Instead of waiting until you have the perfect business plan, all the funding, or every little detail figured out, start taking steps now. Even if you're not heading to the gym, wear clothes that make you feel sporty and active to shift your mindset. It's a reminder to move more and take care of your body.

In many ways, we can be our own worst enemy. We are confined by our own perceptions, constrained by our understanding of true and false. Challenge your own understanding. Test new ideas. There is always room for growth.

This mindset hack has completely changed the way I approach life, business, work, relationships, etc.

When you think about what you want to achieve (with your wellness, your business, your career or relationships) what stands in your way of achieving it now?

Acting as if your beliefs are true is a behavioral approach to overcoming your limiting beliefs. Even if you don't feel different yet, act as if you are. Start doing the things that your healthier, more confident, and more balanced self would do.

When you think about your limiting beliefs, think about all the things you would do differently and how you would live your life if you believed the opposite of that thing!

When you begin to act as if they're true, your mind may not be there, but you will start to see the positive effect of your new habits and behaviors.

Eventually, you'll prove yourself wrong about those beliefs.

Flip the Script

Instead of saying…

"I don't have the time," say, "It's not a priority right now."

"I should or have to _____," say, "I get to _____."

"I feel guilty because _____," say, " I deserve to _____."

Easy Actions to Improve Your Mindset

Just like buying certain foods makes it easier to stick to healthy eating, you can set yourself up physically, mentally, and emotionally to make it easier to maintain a growth mindset.

Now, this isn't a one-and-done or overnight process (just like anything worth doing). It can take some practice and intentional effort to improve your mindset. There are a couple of actions you can take to help make it a little easier as you do so.

Get More Sleep

"I'll sleep when I'm dead."

Have you heard or said this before?

Unfortunately, that's exactly what will happen if you neglect it. Sleep is greatly undervalued for all the benefits it provides.

Studies have shown that a good night's sleep can improve memory, increase productivity, and help us succeed in our daily tasks. Plus, sticking to a regular sleep schedule can reduce your risk of anxiety and depression.

If you find yourself waking up feeling groggy, tired throughout the day, lying awake at night, or relying on caffeine to get you through the day, there's a good chance you're lacking some serious Zzzs. A regular bedtime routine and engaging in relaxing activities at least an hour before bed will help your mind wind down. You can think more clearly and can be more open to learning and exploring options when you're well rested.

Reduce Stress in Your Home

It's normal to experience stress—everybody does. However, it can have negative physical, mental, and emotional side effects when it is excessive, constant, and chronic.

Chronic stress contributes to mood disorders and anxiety and alters areas of the brain involved in memory and critical thinking. Stress decreases our engagement in learning and our ability to remember things. It also increases the time it can take to gain new knowledge.

Reduce stress by turning your home into your end-of-the-day sanctuary (even if it's just one small corner to yourself) to help your mind de-stress and recharge. You will learn more about how to do this as one of the pillars of your self-care practice. For instance, consider decluttering your home for greater mental clarity and setting up a serene environment with nature-related decorations like live plants, leaf patterns, photographs of nature, and landscape paintings. Several studies have shown a link between natural environments and reduced stress levels.

Take Care of Your Body

Just as your body benefits from exercise and healthy eating, so does your brain. Participating in physical activity is one of the best ways to relieve stress and boost your energy for better learning. Studies have shown that any exercise that increases your heart rate has a positive effect on your brain, improving memory, and fighting symptoms of depression.

Maintaining a healthy diet also plays a key role in regulating emotions and brain function.

When you hear this, you may jump to, *"But I don't have time to go to the gym every day,"* or, *"I don't have time to plan meals—we're a busy family."*

I get it—taking care of your body can seem overwhelming. Reframe what this looks like and decide how much time you really need to change your mindset. In the next chapter, we'll talk more about your time concerns and how to address those.

Schedule Some "Me" Time

Making time for yourself is important, but that doesn't mean you necessarily have to be alone. Time for yourself can mean engaging in activities that you enjoy—either on your own or with friends.

Learning new things can help you harness your ability to improve at anything when you put in the effort to support a growth mindset. This increases your confidence and prevents you from engaging in negative self-judgment and giving up when you encounter setbacks.

When the kids were little, we thought it would be fun to teach them to ski. My husband grew up skiing and I didn't, but thought if the kids could learn, so could I. We rented all the gear and headed out to the slopes. I was definitely the oldest one in our lesson group but really wanted to learn how to ski. I was scared every time I picked up speed (sometimes I threw myself on the ground just to slow down!), but I stuck with it. I had more than my fair share of wipeouts, and though the kids picked it up faster and took off down bigger hills, I kept at it. I can now make it down just about every hill (except for some double black diamonds) and have enjoyed many weekends on the slopes with my family.

Practice Daily Gratitude

If you've been in my world at all, you might know that I consider gratitude a powerful but underutilized form of self-care. In 2005, I read about a study on the benefits of gratitude (and Oprah had talked about a daily gratitude practice on her talk show, where she simply wrote five things each day).

I thought, "I can do that." I left a plain, lined notebook on my nightstand and each night would try to come up with my own list of five things I was grateful for. At first, I couldn't always come up with five things—sometimes I could only come up with three. These weren't big things—some days, it was the sun being out, or someone holding the door open for me, or my favorite banana smoothie. Over time, the practice became easier and I was able to list five more consistently.

Take action and start noticing the things that make you feel grateful. It's easy to think about the things that went wrong or the things you don't have (like I said, we're pre-programmed). Over time, as you build this practice, you'll notice it becoming more natural and automatic.

There is actually science behind this, which has to do with our reticular activating system (RAS). The RAS, is a bundle of nerves at our brainstem that filters out unnecessary information so the important stuff gets through. It's why when you're thinking about buying a red car, all of a sudden, you start to see red cars everywhere. There aren't more of them, you're just more aware of them. So if you start to focus on positive thoughts and outcomes you will start to see more of those as well.

To begin your own gratitude practice, acknowledge the things or the people in your life you're grateful for each day. Keep a tiny notepad near your bed or use the notes app on your phone to write down three to five things you are grateful for each day—the small things that make you smile. As you practice gratitude consistently, you'll not only notice the positive more in each day, but you'll override negative thoughts (or limiting beliefs) that can pop up.

Time to Put it into Practice!

We talked about mindset and ways to master your mindset, so now let's practice with a mindset exercise to start changing the way you think.

Think of a situation in which you weren't able to reach your goal or one that didn't have the outcome you expected. Explore the details of what happened. What were your reactions or emotions to the event? Did you feel frustrated? Discouraged? Angry? Hurt?

Now, think of the situation in a different light that allows more possibility for that goal to be achieved in the future.

How could your feelings about the situation be different?

_____

_____

What's one new concept you can learn?

_____

_____

Is there a way to change how you approach the situation?

_____

_____

Write down one to three ways you can learn something new about this:

_____

_____

_____

_____

Chapter 5

Designing Your Day

*"You will never FIND time for anything. If
you want time you must make it."*

— Charles Buxton

Why Is Time Planning Important?

So now that we've worked on changing the way you think about
your day, let's change the way you feel about it by giving you control
over how you're spending your time.

In the hustle and bustle of your daily life, being intentional about
what you're spending your time on each day can get lost. Picture
this: You're juggling work, family commitments, personal projects,
and maybe adding a smidgen of self-care. Without a well-thought-
out time plan, unfortunately, self-care is usually the first thing to go

(even though we need it), and packing your day with everything else can leave you feeling exhausted and destined for burnout city.

Here's the scoop: Effective time planning isn't just about ticking off tasks on your to-do list. It's your key to reclaiming control over your day, your week—heck, your whole life. When you master the art of intentionally planning your time, you're not just managing minutes and hours; you're crafting a roadmap to overall well-being.

A principle called Parkinson's Law states, "Work expands to fill the time allotted." Put simply, the amount of time a task requires adjusts to the time available for you to complete it.

So, for example, if you wait until the last minute for a project, it may only take a couple of hours to do, but if you give yourself three days, it will take you three days.

It all comes down to the same thing—the longer we put something off, the longer it takes before you complete it.

On the other hand, creating space to excel in your passions while protecting precious moments for self-care is like giving yourself permission to thrive without sacrificing your sanity.

Think about it: When you carve out dedicated slots for work, relaxation, socializing and sleep, you're essentially saying, "Hey, I've got this!"

The beauty of effective time planning is in the ripple effect it has on your overall well-being. By being intentional about how you spend your time, you lay the groundwork for reduced stress, increased productivity, and a deeper sense of fulfillment. It's not just about getting stuff done; it's about living a life where balance isn't a dream, but a daily reality.

Common Myths About Your Time

Do you believe the same "time" myths many others think are true? Let's take a look.

The first myth is believing you can actually "manage" your time. While you can set schedules and prioritize tasks, unexpected events, distractions, and varying levels of productivity can throw off the best-laid plans. This is why I call this pillar of the formula "time planning" rather than time management because it's not just about playing defense and managing whatever comes along. Rather, it's about intentionally prioritizing and deciding your schedule.

When you think about time in this way, it becomes something you respect and craft in the way you want to. Instead of striving for perfect time management, it's more realistic to focus on adaptability and resilience. Acknowledging that time management is a continual learning process helps adjust expectations and develop strategies that work best for individual circumstances.

The next myth: You believe buying a new planner is the solution. The planner is not the solution. It's a great tool to help you organize the items in your day, but the fact that your time is disorganized and out of control has nothing to do with the tool. It's *you*.

So, while a well-designed planner can certainly be a helpful tool, it's not a magic solution on its own. A new planner won't address underlying issues such as procrastination, lack of prioritization, or unrealistic goal-setting. It's essential to combine the use of a planner with strategies like setting clear goals, breaking tasks into manageable steps, scheduling regular reviews, and practicing self-discipline (which we will talk more about later in the chapter).

Another myth is that scheduling your time will mean your life is too rigid or restrictive and no fun at all. Putting boundaries on your time actually gives you freedom: freedom to relax and not worry that you're forgetting something, and freedom to say yes to things you want to do because you know whether you have time for it.

Having a schedule allows you to prioritize important tasks, allocate time for self-care, access leisure activities, and stay organized. A schedule can also help you avoid procrastination and reduce stress by breaking down large tasks into smaller, manageable chunks. You can also decrease stress by intentionally incorporating buffer times between tasks in case of unexpected events or delays.

Another myth is that there's one "right" way to manage your time. Everyone's tasks and personal style are unique and highly individualized. So, how you set up your day can vary greatly, depending on personality, lifestyle, priorities, and goals. What works well for one person may not be suitable for another. The key involves finding an approach that aligns with your unique style.

Some individuals thrive on detailed schedules and strict routines, while others are more boho and flexible. Experimenting with different techniques, such as time blocking, prioritization strategies, task batching, or using digital tools, can help you discover what works best for you. I'll explain how to do these in more depth later in the chapter.

The final myth: You'll eventually be done with everything on your to-do list. The reality is that tasks, responsibilities, and goals are often ongoing and dynamic. Life constantly evolves, presenting new challenges, opportunities, and priorities. As soon as you cross off one task, another takes its place. It's important to recognize that having an endless to-do list is not a sign of failure, but rather, a reflection of real life. Instead of striving for completion, focus on prioritizing tasks based on their importance and impact. Learn to delegate or let go of tasks that aren't essential, or that someone else can handle.

Take Control of Your Time Planning

Time is the one thing that everyone feels they never have enough of, want to manage better, and can never really get a handle on.

It's kind of ironic how time management at work is a crucial component of project management, collaboration, and independent work. While many of you may be good at this professionally, you may have a hard time carrying it over to your personal lives.

People also have a tough time recognizing when they're wasting time. They force themselves to sit at their desk for hours or to fiddle around with changing the fonts on a presentation. But there comes a time when you will become less productive than if you would just take a break.

Start understanding what stands in your way. Plan your time in a way that feels good to you. When you catch yourself scrolling on social media, stop, grab some water, and take some deep breaths. You might be taking on too many tasks or working when your body is at low energy.

When you feel exhausted but feel the need to check your email one more time, remember the boundaries that you have (hopefully) clearly communicated and show yourself respect. If it's hard for you to do, find an accountability partner to get the support you may need to stay consistent.

It may not be easy at first, but eventually,with consistency, you'll start to change your schedule and incorporate consistent habits so you're optimizing your time. These may include:

- Eating, sleeping, and working at regular (or at least semi-regular) intervals
- Making lists of what is a priority each day, setting break times to let yourself refocus, and moving around throughout the day to keep yourself alert.

For those who appreciate structure (talking to you, my Listers), this may be your best form of self-care.

For example, have you ever had a reactive, stressful response at seeing the laundry pile up and get stressed and overwhelmed that it's there? Have you ever spent the better part of a day running cycle after cycle of laundry, regardless of the other things you'd initially planned?

The calmer, more intentional response involves anticipating a load of laundry and scheduling a time to make it happen. Regardless of how high you see the pile getting, you know you've worked laundry into your schedule.

Now, I get that unexpected things can and will pop up every single day. But you can add routine, day-to-day tasks into your schedule.

Scheduling routine chores into your day and week doesn't mean that you suddenly do laundry every single day; however, it does mean that you have a plan to tackle the laundry and stay in control of when you choose to deal with it.

That's why prioritizing and planning your days is such a foundational piece of a less stressful life. It helps you slow down and become intentional about where your time goes.

The great thing is there's no such thing as one "right" way to manage time!

I worked with someone who shared that they actually look forward to laundry time because that's when they allow themselves to binge on Netflix. By combining a mindset shift and habit stacking, they created a block of self-care during a necessary activity.

Whether you are super structured or a bit more boho and laid back, you can tap into a strategy that aligns with your goals and personality.

It's so easy to walk all over your own boundaries and spend hours and hours in your business, or with your kids, or in your relationship because it's your passion. But there is a difference between *busy* and *productive* (not just with tasks, but with people as well!). Becoming more intentional with your time when you are acting on your passion will make it easier to set boundaries so you also allow other things/people onto your calendar. This includes setting priorities so you are present, focused, and not distracted by other things.

But don't just try time management once, find it doesn't work for you, stop it altogether, and then say, "Time management isn't for me." The only way to know what works for you is to try different options until you find the one that does work best for you. It won't be perfect at first (that's why it's called practice), but eventually, you'll start to change and incorporate the structure you need to optimize your time.

Regardless of your style, try time blocking as one key element.

Why Time Blocking Matters

So, why does time blocking matter, anyway? The short version: It helps you protect two extremely precious resources—your time and focus. Our brain is better able to handle smaller segments of data, making it easier to understand, concentrate on and remember complex information.

When distractions and incoming emails direct your workday, productivity goes down the drain. Some data indicates it takes as long as twenty-three minutes on average to regain focus after an interruption.

Time blocking gets you out of defense mode, stops letting tangents ruin your concentration, and starts calling the shots about the type of work you do, and when.

Time blocking offers a few other major benefits:

- **Helps establish flow:** "Flow" is a fluid work state where you focus and work at maximum efficiency. Time blocking helps you achieve a flow state by allowing you to dedicate parts of your day to very specific types of work (and nothing else).
- **Minimizes distraction:** Because time blocking is the opposite of multitasking, it allows for concentration on a single task. This means you have more mental bandwidth to devote to what you're working on, which is good news, as lack of distraction can boost attention to detail and produce fewer errors (and even help you finish quicker).
- **Creates a sense of control:** When we feel more control over what we're doing and when, it helps reduce stress and anxiety. In the short term, time blocking allows you to gain more control over the day, rather than just winging it. In the long term, it allows for more effective planning and decision making.
- **Decreases decision fatigue:** Limiting some of your decision making throughout the day can help lessen overwhelming feelings and can actually make you more productive.

Time blocking also improves focus and deters procrastination. You set aside specific blocks of time to complete important must-do tasks. Time blocking helps you prioritize your tasks, makes your to-do list more manageable, and also gives you more control over your day.

Time Blocking Steps

Here's how to time block:

- **Develop your list.** Brain dump your weekly tasks. Include everything from large to small, regardless of how insignificant something seems. If it takes your time, put it on the list. What are the repetitive tasks you perform every week? Whether it's chores, meetings, activities, or events, they can find a place more seamlessly in your day if you intentionally plan them out (even if you know they're going to keep happening).
- **Determine your priorities.** Based on that list, you need to figure out which ones stay on your calendar. The Eisenhower Matrix tool (see image below) can help you break down tasks into the following categories: important/urgent, important/not urgent, not important/urgent, and not important/not urgent. The items in the "urgent and important" box must happen, and you can even designate which tasks have to happen on a specific day or time, because those are the ones you'll plan first.

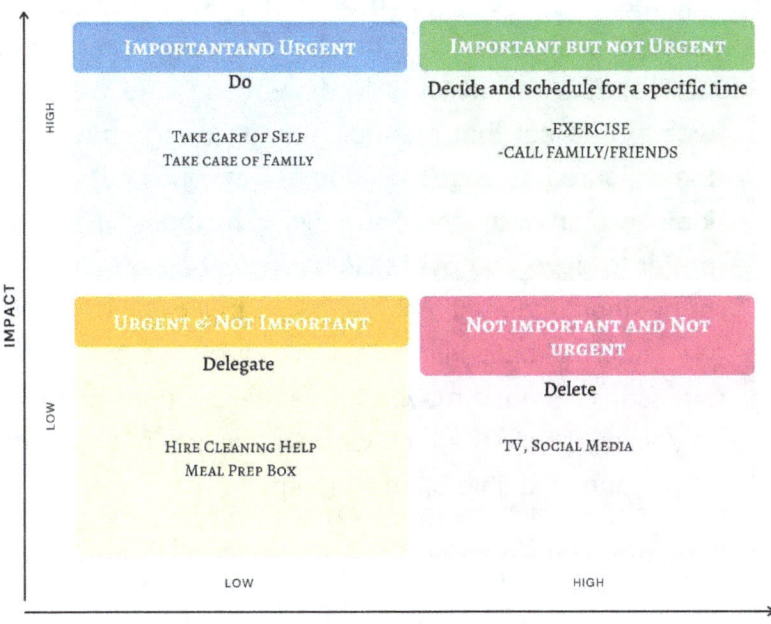

Now, consider the urgent/not important tasks. Which ones can you delegate? For example, maybe you can carpool with another parent to get your child to soccer practice.

Next, go to the last box from your list, those non-urgent, not-important ones, and completely delete them.

Designate specific times for priorities each day so you are present and focused, not distracted by other nonessential tasks. Also consider how you'd like to structure your weeks for maximum productivity. Be realistic as you plan and ask yourself questions about what makes sense on different days. Do you have set meetings on Tuesdays? Is your inbox jam packed on Mondays? Plan accordingly.

- **Estimate how long each task should take.** Put together a rough estimate of how much time you spend doing each task. Be sure to account for how much time you normally waste (and cut that number out). You don't have to have these figured down to the minute—just put together a rough idea to start with and fine-tune from there. If anything, I prefer to have you overestimate how long a task will take, rather than underestimate. Allow for traffic if traveling. When we underestimate things that take time, we can get a little stressed, because maybe it does take longer and we start to spill over onto the time we've allocated for the next task. Give yourself a little bit of extra space.

  Try it out for a couple of days or a week and then adapt it once you see how it works for you. If some tasks look too big, how can you break them down into smaller chunks, spread out over a day or a week? I totally understand you don't always have a choice (like with work meetings), but if you can break things down into smaller chunks, it will make them easier to manage.

- **Block off each day.** Blocking off each day helps you see gaps. Gaps are good, because you'll eventually fit self-care into them. You can also visually see if there is too much overlap, so try to intentionally leave gaps and spaces between tasks. Things will come up, so leave time for miscellaneous tasks and those little surprises that scream, "I gotta take care of this right now!" You could use your flexible time for unplanned tasks and/or meetings that pop up, a coffee date with a friend, a walk outside, ten minutes to read—whatever you want or need it for. You need to prioritize and organize your work, home tasks, and social life without becoming completely exhausted! (I like to add one social/personal block to my calendar to ensure it's there.) Maintaining a healthy flow/harmony between work, home, and personal downtime is no small feat and requires good time planning skills.

- **Protect your time.** As you think this over, consider the type of organization you work in and what their expectations might be. Maintaining boundaries within the context of the organization's expectations can be really hard, especially when you have kids, a job, and maybe even some people-pleasing tendencies. Consider where you work, the people in your life (and their expectations), how you can communicate your work responsibilities, how you'll spend your time, and your boundaries.

  For example, maybe you want to check emails only up to 4 p.m. Consider sending an auto-reply email after 4 p.m. that says something like, "Hey, I'm so glad you reached out to me. I'll get back to you in the morning..." It'll alleviate your stress and communicate when you'll get back to individuals.

  Do people usually schedule time with you in advance? If so, set specific start and end times to help you maintain your boundaries.

  Are you expected to have a certain amount of availability to others? Clearly communicating these hours will also help you allot time more realistically and relieve guilt that you're not constantly available to them.

- **Review your plan.** Do your allocated times exceed your waking or working hours? Take a minute to review your list. Identify how you've broken down your time and your priorities, and where things fall. You might go through busy seasons at work, and your kids' sports might take up more time. Ensure that your plan has the flow and flexibility you need to plan for these busy seasons, and adjust accordingly. Reviewing your schedule isn't a one-and-done process, either. Let your time-blocked schedule evolve over time. If your work changes with the season or time of year, you may need to do monthly or quarterly reviews. Taking the time to do each step will help you build the habit and muscle memory so it becomes natural before you know it.

Now that you've gone through the basic time blocking concept and steps, you might look at your days and weeks and think, now what?

It's not just enough to have the items scheduled on your calendar—you also need a plan to effectively execute and complete the tasks.

Get a Calendar and Use It!

Find a suitable calendar that works for you and use it, whether it's a paper planner, a digital calendar, or a big month-at-a-glance wall calendar. It doesn't matter what you choose—get whatever feels right for you.

Next, write everything down! Write it down so you can see your schedule and plan ahead. It might seem so elementary, but it'll surprise you to see how much easier things are when you aren't carrying the mental load of remembering your entire schedule.

Next, what stands in the way of your time management? Too much social media? Taking on too many tasks? Or working when your body is at low energy?

Using your calendar won't be perfect at first as you may still get distracted by breaks or inconsistency, but eventually, you'll start to change your schedule and incorporate consistent habits so you optimize your time to help yourself and everyone around you.

Impacts of Procrastination

Even the best plans can get tripped up.

Procrastination often keeps people from completing the tasks on their list. Subconscious procrastination can often hinder our progress in achieving tasks without even realizing it. This form of procrastination manifests as subtle avoidance behaviors, excuses, or distractions that prevent us from taking meaningful action.

Procrastination can stem from fear of failure, perfectionism, feeling overwhelmed, or a lack of clear goals. One effective way to overcome procrastination involves breaking tasks down into smaller, more manageable chunks. This approach makes tasks feel more achievable. Start by identifying the specific steps or actions required to complete a task and then focus on tackling them, one step at a time.

Set realistic deadlines for each sub-task and hold yourself accountable. Celebrate small victories along the way to stay motivated and build momentum. By addressing subconscious procrastination through systematic task breakdown, you can increase productivity, boost confidence, and move closer to achieving your goals.

The Pomodoro Technique is an excellent component in a successful time management plan, especially effective against procrastination, where typically the biggest obstacle is just getting started. Each "pomodoro" interval (named after the tomato-shaped timer the guy who invented it used) sets a number of minutes for a task and then sets a timed break. This break gives you a chance to rest, recharge, and reset to bring your attention back to your work. The method can help you resist the self-interruptions and subconscious procrastination that can keep us from achieving our tasks. It can also help retrain your brain to focus, and can gradually help you increase the length of time you are able to do so.

For example, you might work for twenty-five minutes, then take a five-minute break. This technique also helps overcome procrastination by breaking things down into smaller, manageable chunks.

Overall, managing our schedules effectively is crucial for balancing our responsibilities and achieving our goals. By setting priorities, creating realistic schedules, and staying organized, we can make the most of our time and reduce stress.

Chapter 6

Thrive with Self-Care

"Self-care is not self-indulgence, it is self-preservation."

— Audre Lorde

Self-care, shmelf-care...

Unfortunately, the term "self-care" has become so overused in our society that we've become "ear-blind." It's just another glossed-over buzzword.

Self-care might seem like fluff, and you might think, "I already know that," or "I don't have the time, money, or energy to do it."

Well, that stops *now*.

You need to reclaim self-care as an essential part of who you are and how you operate.

Every.

Single.

Day.

You might be thinking "Sure, I've heard that before..." and you know what? Together, we're gonna make it happen.

I'm not talking about an occasional luxury like a spa day or a weekend away (even though I love these!), but daily, *practical* self-care actions. Self-care is any activity done deliberately to take care of your own mental, emotional, and physical health. It's as simple as taking time to prioritize anything that benefits your own personal well-being, which provides benefits to everyone around you.

Why Self-Care Matters

Imagine you're driving down the road with a rock in your tire. You might still be able to drive, but you feel the "thud" of that stone every time it hits the road.

That's what it's like when one of your self-care areas is out of alignment. You still get by each day, but it just doesn't feel right. When you master consistent self-care, you give yourself a smoother life ride.

Real self-care does not come from occasional luxuries or pampering, but rather intentional systems around money, sleep, relationships, style, organization, movement, food, and more!

Self-care becomes a way of life, especially how you present and believe in yourself. It's something you should do every day. It's about building a whole system of routines and habits that help create a lifestyle you love.

Without regular daily self-care, you're likely to end up feeling stressed, tired, and generally unmotivated, regardless of what you're doing. While it can be something that we often neglect or put off, it's critical for our physical, mental, and emotional well-being.

Self-care matters because:

- We can improve our overall physical well-being by taking care of ourselves through exercise, healthy eating habits, and proper sleep. Self-care can lead to increased energy levels, improved concentration, and a more positive outlook on life.
- Taking time for ourselves and engaging in activities that we enjoy can help reduce stress and anxiety, improve our mood, and boost our self-esteem. It can also help us develop resilience and cope with life's challenges.
- Self-care allows us to tune in to our emotions and needs and to be kinder to ourselves. By practicing self-care, we can develop a greater sense of self-awareness and self-acceptance, which can lead to more fulfilling relationships with ourselves and others.

What's at Stake?

So, let's look at how self-care can negatively affect you, as well as some signs that indicate you need more self-care in your life.

Stress and Exhaustion

When you don't take care of yourself, you may feel stressed and exhausted, which can lead to burnout and resentment. For example, you might feel exhausted from taking care of everyone else's needs. If you don't take time for self-care, you could end up resenting your loved ones over time. When you're constantly exhausted and stressed, it might feel difficult to maintain a positive outlook.

Mental Wellness

Not following a daily self-care routine can impact your overall mental wellness. Self-care activities make you feel good physically and mentally, improving your resilience to handle all of life's ups and downs. When you neglect your self-care, you may feel less able to bounce back from negative events in your life.

Unhealthy Habits

When you lack self-care, you can easily fall into unhealthy habits, like overworking at all hours or overindulging in junk food because it's quick and easy, or turning to alcohol or drugs to cope with stress and daily life. When you turn to unhealthy habits for comfort, it could lead to other problems in other areas.

Self-Doubt

If you fail to take care of yourself, you can end up feeling like you're never good enough. When you're constantly overwhelmed and exhausted from juggling life's responsibilities, you may feel like a failure, or that you simply don't measure up to others.

These are just some of the things that can happen when you don't include a self-care routine in your daily life. The effects can cause you to lead an unhappy and unfulfilled life.

Self-care is something you do because you're worth it! It's not something you need to "earn" or "deserve." It helps you build confidence and optimism and build positive self-talk and mindset skills.

Adding self-care to your day doesn't need to take a lot of time or cost a lot of money. It's about finding what works for you and doing it consistently every day. It might change each day and will look different for everyone.

I'm giving you permission to start focusing on your needs and making self-care a priority *right now*!

Common Self-Care Pitfalls

Just like eating a lettuce-only diet isn't necessarily healthy, focusing too heavily in one area of your life and neglecting other areas will definitely make you feel out of alignment (like focusing only on your job or the gym and ignoring everything else).

Here are some ways you can sabotage your self-care practice. Do any of these seem familiar?

- **Inconsistency:** One of the most common pitfalls is inconsistent self-care practices. Inconsistency includes skipping your self-care activities when your calendar gets full, or neglecting self-care during stressful times. Consistency is the key to reaping self-care benefits. For example, I keep my regular morning and evening routines, but vary my workout length (because ten minutes of yoga versus no yoga is a win).
- **Not prioritizing self-care:** Many people prioritize other responsibilities (such as work, family obligations, or social activities) over self-care. But you don't show up as your best self in all other areas you deem "more important" if you don't make self-care a priority.
- **Setting unrealistic expectations:** You might expect self-care activities to completely eliminate stress, or expect immediate results from self-care practices. It's important to have realistic expectations and understand that self-care is an ongoing process. Realistic results might look like not having an extreme emotional reaction every time something doesn't go according to plan, like when I taught my daughter to drive and didn't freak out when she took a turn too fast.
- **Using self-care as an escape:** While self-care is important for managing stress and promoting well-being, it's possible to use it to avoid dealing with underlying issues or responsibilities. It's essential to address the root causes of your stress. For example, you might stay in a toxic relationship or ignore a heart attack or mental health diagnosis, but still maintain your self-care routine. It's a

pitfall to assume that you're taking care of yourself in these situations, so seek professional support if needed. Self-care is just a *part* of staying well.

- **Comparison:** Comparing your self-care practices or achievements to others can lead to feelings of inadequacy or pressure to meet unrealistic standards. It's important to focus on what works best for you and tailor your self-care routine to your individual needs and preferences.

- **Overloading self-care activities:** Starting too many self-care activities at once or overwhelming yourself with elaborate self-care routines can backfire because it's too hard to keep up with. Start with small, manageable steps and gradually incorporate more self-care practices as needed.

- **Guilt:** Many of us feel guilty for taking time for ourselves, especially if it means saying "no" to others or taking time away from work. However, it's important to remember that self-care is not selfish and equips us to take care of others and perform our best.

- **Lack of resources:** Lack of resources can mean you have diminished financial resources. For example, you might not have the cash to buy a gym membership. However, you can tap into free online resources, public spaces for exercise, and creative solutions to accommodate your budget.

- **Social expectations:** We may feel pressure to always be productive and prioritize work over our personal lives. However, it's important to remember to put your well-being first, and that it's okay to take breaks.

Finding a balance that works for you and incorporating self-care into your daily routine can promote overall well-being and resilience.

Optimize Your Day for Self-Care

You can incorporate more self-care in your life in just a couple of minutes each day.

First, "unplug" from work. So many jobs no longer require a nine-to-five office routine, but accessibility to phones and laptops means we often end up working more hours than a typical workday. Set clear boundaries for your start time, lunchtime, short breaks, and end time. Eat your meal away from your desk or usual work spot. If you can, shut the door to your office during off-hours or cover your computer. Also, don't check emails outside of work hours.

The second tip has to do with your task and time management. Each day, have a plan for what you need to do. Use strategies like the Eisenhower Matrix or the Pomodoro Technique.

Lastly, choose some quick self-care activities ahead of time that have a significant effect on mental and physical health. Too often, when we get free time but no plan, we default to aimlessly scrolling on our phones. The activities you choose can include:

- A one-minute mindful breath and water break (set a timer to go off five times a day to prompt you)
- A ten-minute walk (preferably outside) during your lunch hour
- Connecting with a friend or listening to a book/podcast on your commute
- Ten minutes of yoga or meditation (many free guided ones on YouTube), laughing daily (alone or with others)
- Decorating and organizing in a way that makes you calm and brings joy so you can relax at home, even if it's just a small corner of your living room

Want more ideas? Grab a free resource on my website: "Reclaim Your Time in 10-Minute Blocks Cheat Sheet" with 20+ ideas for carving out the space you need and what to do with it.

Taking action before (or when) you experience burnout can protect your overall mental health. By taking the time to be intentional with the structure of your day and the actions you choose to incorporate, you can create regular routines to rest and relax at home. There's no right or wrong way to engage in self-care as long as it's intentional and makes you feel good about yourself.

What is Practical Self-Care?

Real, sustainable self-care doesn't mean just taking advantage of occasional luxuries or pampering, but rather, intentional daily systems I like to call "Practical Self-Care."

So, what is it?

It's a way of living and presenting yourself and believing in yourself all the time.

Practical Self-Care is a system of routines and habits woven into your day-to-day life that helps create a lifestyle that you love.

The system I teach involves eight pillars:

- Sleep
- Eat
- Think about money

- Connect with others
- Dress
- Decorate/organize your home
- Move your body
- Engage in traditional personal development like journaling, meditation, mindfulness, etc.

In the rest of this chapter, we'll dive deeper into the individual pillars to show how they benefit your work/life balance and overall wellness. We'll also present you with some beginning action steps to integrate into your life.

1. Sleep Habits

There are so many demands on our time—jobs, family, etc., not to mention the need to find some time for yourself. Unfortunately, you might short yourself on sleep to fit it all in.

From pulling all-nighters in college to burning the midnight oil to get ahead professionally, to having kids (especially young ones), the lack of sleep that can come with it can take a serious toll, because the amount and quality of your sleep affects your mental and physical health.

Sleep is so much more than something you do to help yourself feel rested each day. While you're sleeping, your brain and body consciously shut down, but so many restorative processes occur. You might've heard someone who didn't get a good night's sleep say, "I feel like I've been hit by a truck," because their body didn't have a chance to repair itself overnight and prepare for the day ahead.

Sleep allows your body to repair and recharge, improve your cognitive functioning, regulate mood, and strengthen your immune system. Not getting quality sleep can contribute to everything from weight gain, to energy loss, to lack of productivity. Making sleep a priority in your self-care routine not only improves your overall health and well-being, but also enhances your productivity, mood, and ability to cope with daily stressors.

It's not just about the quantity of sleep, but also the quality. Sometimes it can be hard to fall asleep—or if you're like me, you can fall asleep but struggle to *stay* asleep. (Do you wake up at the same time every night (*Hello, 3 a.m.!*) like me?)

While everyone talks about morning routines, set yourself up for success the next day by having a solid bedtime routine.

In my case, I start with my skincare routine of washing and moisturizing my face, getting into my jammies, moisturizing my lips and feet, and then reading (from an actual book). Even if I only read a couple of pages, the whole routine stays the same, even if the length of time varies.

Here are some action steps you can take to improve your sleep as part of your self-care routine:

- **Establish a consistent sleep schedule:** Go to bed and wake up at the same time every day, even on weekends, to regulate your body's internal clock.
- **Create a relaxing bedtime routine:** Develop a soothing bedtime routine that includes activities like reading a book,

taking a warm bath, practicing relaxation exercises (deep breathing, stretching, or listening to calming music).

- **Create a comfortable sleep environment:** Ensure your bedroom is conducive to sleep by keeping it cool, dark, and quiet. Invest in a comfortable mattress and pillows that support your sleep posture.
- **Limit stimulants and electronics:** Avoid caffeine, nicotine, and heavy meals close to bedtime. Limit screen time on electronic devices like smartphones, tablets, and computers to at least an hour before bed.
- **Regular exercise:** Engage in regular physical activity during the day, but avoid intense exercise close to bedtime. Exercise can promote better sleep quality and help regulate your sleep-wake cycle.
- **Mindful eating:** Be mindful of what and when you eat, especially in the hours leading up to bedtime. Avoid heavy or spicy foods that may cause discomfort or indigestion before you plan to sleep.
- **Manage stress and anxiety:** Practice stress-reducing techniques such as deep breathing, meditation, yoga, or journaling to calm your mind and reduce nighttime worries.
- **Limit daytime naps:** If you nap during the day, keep it short (around twenty to thirty minutes) and avoid napping too close to bedtime to prevent disrupting nighttime sleep.
- **Seek professional help if needed:** If you have persistent sleep issues or suspect a sleep disorder, consult with a healthcare professional or sleep specialist for evaluation and guidance.

2. Eating Habits

Food: It's such a loaded topic!

Everyone has an opinion about which diet is best (Mediterranean, paleo, keto… it's an endless list). Food can bring people together in celebration and can be used as a way to manage stress (whether you devour endless pints of ice cream to escape the sadness of a breakup, or, like me when I'm tired, crave carbs all day long).

What we put in our bodies affects our health, energy level, immunity, and how we show up in our daily lives.

I hear so many people say that they know meal planning makes sense. But they also say, "It's too much work," or "We don't have the time," or "It's too restrictive," or "My family won't be on board."

Does any of this sound familiar?

Eating healthy doesn't have to be a chore. Here are some action steps you can take to incorporate healthy eating habits into your self-care routine:

- **Meal plan:** Dedicate time each week to plan and prep your meals and snacks (many people I work with love to do this on Sundays). Create a grocery list based on what you know you and your family will actually eat (there's nothing worse than throwing out a whole produce drawer of healthy food that no one wants). Choose foods like fruits, vegetables, whole grains, lean proteins, and healthy fats. No, you don't have to eliminate healthy fats; just use moderation and grace.

- **Cook at home:** Try to cook at home more often, using fresh ingredients. Experiment with new recipes and cooking techniques to make meal preparation enjoyable and exciting. If you're strapped for time, meal services like Hello Fresh or Blue Apron enable you to still cook at home—they just do the meal planning and shopping for you.
- **Mindful eating:** Practice mindful eating by slowing down during meals, chewing your food thoroughly, and paying attention to hunger and fullness cues. You can do this more easily when you step away from your desk, computer, or phone during meals. (The "clean plate club" I grew up with was *not* a great idea.)
- **Hydrate:** Drink an adequate amount of water throughout the day to stay hydrated. Limit sugary beverages like juice, pop, and alcohol. Opt for water, herbal teas, or infused water instead.
- **Balanced plate:** Aim for a balanced plate at each meal, including a variety of colors (watch out for "beige plates") and food groups. Fill half your plate with vegetables, a quarter with lean protein, and a quarter with whole grains or starchy vegetables.
- **Healthy snacks:** Keep healthy snacks on hand, such as fresh fruit, nuts, yogurt, or whole-grain crackers, to make nutritious choices easy to grab and go. When I meal prep, I also cut up carrots, celery, and other snacks so it's easier to make decisions about what to eat when hunger strikes.
- **Portion control:** Be mindful of portion sizes to avoid overeating. Use smaller plates and bowls, and again, listen to your body's hunger and fullness signals.

- **Limit processed foods:** Reduce your intake of processed foods high in added sugars, sodium, and unhealthy fats. Choose minimally processed foods whenever possible.
- **Practice moderation:** Allow yourself to enjoy treats or indulgent foods in moderation, without guilt or restriction. Balance indulgence with nourishing options in your overall diet.
- **Seek professional guidance:** I am *not* a dietician or nutritionist, and everyone has different needs and medical requirements. If you have specific dietary concerns or health goals, consider consulting with a registered dietitian or nutritionist for personalized guidance—support is a *must* before diving into any new program.

3. Money

Here's one often-overlooked component of self-care: money. Believe it or not, finding ways to build financial self-care into your daily routine can have a profound effect on your overall well-being and happiness.

Our financial situations can have a major impact on our mental health and overall happiness. A 2020 survey by Bankrate found that 48% of U.S. adults lose sleep over money worries, particularly everyday expenses, followed by retirement savings and healthcare or insurance bills.

It's really hard to focus on relaxing or self-care when you're worried about paying your bills.

But money doesn't just affect your mind. Financial struggles result in physical consequences, too. Stressing over money can cause high blood pressure, stomach issues, headaches, and even increase the risk of stroke. Not having enough money can also mean you can't afford important health procedures, medications, or nutritious foods.

Practicing financial self-care means developing habits that work for you and reflect what you're trying to achieve with your money. Money habits can vary for different people, but you must apply them consistently. Bad money habits can get in the way of financial self-care, like:

Bad money habits stand in the way of financial self-care. When we're stressed about money we might avoid the topic and go watch TV or, even worse, go shopping. By being aware of our triggers and how we cope, we can choose to take more deliberate actions, such as reviewing our budget or financial statements.

Financial trauma is a real thing, and if avoidance is your coping mechanism, it's time to tackle the beast head-on.

Creating a weekly financial self-care routine can help promote good money habits. Some simple ways to start include:

- **Creating a budget.** Setting clear financial goals can help you get motivated to develop and stick to good money habits. Go over your budget regularly. Schedule a quiet time to imagine and write down your top two short- and long-term financial goals. Vividly describe your goals. What steps will you take to achieve them? Picture yourself reaching them and say them out loud. Be as descriptive as possible. Make your desires concrete by spelling out the details: your target dollar amount, deadlines, and milestones to reach along the way.

- **Track your spending.** Check your bank accounts once a week. Mastering your money means having a clear sense of how it comes in or goes out. Make a daily habit of checking in with your spending, at least until you get a handle on your habits. Be realistic about how you budget and save.

- **Review bill due dates and payments.** Save time paying bills by automating your bill payments. You can automate with a powerful expense-tracking app or keep a simple spreadsheet or jot down notes with paper and a pencil. Seeing the dollars and cents and knowing exactly where your money goes can help you quickly start to feel more in control.

- **Give yourself grace.** If you have less-than-perfect money management skills or you don't reach every milestone, give yourself a break. Take stock of your accomplishments with financial self-care activities and keep putting one foot in front of the other. The well-balanced money life you've been striving for will soon be right in front of you.

- **Set goals for your future spending habits.** The stronger you feel about attaining something (an important certification, a better job, money for the holidays, a savings goal), the more likely you'll remain committed over the long run.

- **Start an emergency fund.** If you have your spending in check, something set aside for emergencies, money left over after saving for retirement—pat yourself on the back. You've worked hard to get to this point. Much of the stress you feel today may be coming from worrying about tomorrow.

- **Talk about money.** A USA Today study found that 70% of people don't talk about everyday financial issues, and more than a quarter admit to hiding debt from their partner. You should never feel ashamed and alone in your struggle to manage money. If you need personalized attention and service (and don't mind paying for it), enlist a financial advisor. Many offer free initial consultations or charge only a small flat fee.

So ditch the guilt and find a supportive friend or consider scheduling a money date with your partner to discuss your budget. Stop pretending everything is fine and bring your money worries, hopes, and dreams into the light of day.

4. Connecting with Others

Supportive relationships have a major impact on our health and well-being. In fact, we need close relationships in order to thrive—it's one of the clearest findings to emerge from happiness research. You should always have people to help you celebrate the good times and provide support through the bad times. Other people and close friendships even help us live longer!

Research has credited friendship and social connection with:

- Boosting happiness
- Reducing stress and stress-related health problems
- Increasing a sense of belonging, connection, and purpose
- Lowering risk of mental illness
- Improving self-worth

- Helping cope with traumas, such as divorce, serious illness, job loss, or the death of a loved one
- Encouraging healthy lifestyle habits, such as exercise or quitting smoking
- Promoting growth and learning
- Providing fun

Having a strong social network may positively affect your physical health by improving sleep, impulse control, stress, and blood pressure.

The amount of social connection a person needs to feel fulfilled may vary depending on the individual, but contrary to popular belief, introverts and extroverts benefit equally from good relationships, though the size and quality of their social network may differ. Some people prefer a large and diverse network of social connections, while others benefit from having a few close friendships.

Introverts (or those of us with introverted tendencies) tend to recharge by spending time alone. They lose energy from being around people for long periods of time, particularly large crowds. Extroverts, on the other hand, derive energy from other people.

Fostering Healthy Relationships

You can foster healthy relationships in a few key ways:

- **Set boundaries:** The key is finding a balance between socializing enough, but not too much. It's okay to take a break and plan some intentional time for yourself.

- **Reach out to others:** Maintaining social relationships takes time and effort, from both sides. While it's great to be the one saying yes to social invitations, it's also good to take the initiative to reach out to others, too. Be intentional with who you reach out to. Put time into relationships that recharge you, add value to your life, and leave you feeling fulfilled.
- **Quality over quantity:** Surface-level interactions with others isn't the same as social self-care—it's more than having brief meetings with people. These relationships are meant to be a part of your self-care, so they should make you feel good. Enjoying meaningful conversations and activities so you get the quality time you need within those friendships.
- **Get creative:** Make it fun! Incorporate your hobbies into your social interactions. For example, if you like to read, you could start a book club; if you like to cook, you could make dinners together. If you like to exercise, you could go on walks or hikes with friends. Consider sharing the activities you enjoy as a part of your self-care with others.
- **Use technology for good:** You can keep in touch with social media, video chat, phone calls, and text messaging. While these don't substitute meaningful face-to-face interactions, they keep us connected. Maintain healthy boundaries like you would in real life, such as unfollowing unhealthy relationships and limiting your time online.
- **Get a pet:** A pet can serve as a good source of companionship and unconditional love. Pets can also facilitate human social relationships. Pets provide the opportunities to get outside, meet other people, interact with other pet owners, and can help us form new friendships.

- **Meet new people:** Increase your opportunities to interact with others by joining clubs, attending festivals and concerts, or by volunteering at an organization with a cause you care about. You can also use apps and websites to meet others either in a group setting or one-on-one. Or meet people spontaneously—the next time you wait in line or run into your neighbor, strike up a casual conversation.

5. Movement

Regular physical activity has numerous benefits, including improving cardiovascular health, strengthening muscles and bones, boosting mood, reducing stress, and enhancing overall energy levels. Movement not only supports your physical fitness, but also plays a significant role in maintaining a positive outlook and improving cognitive function.

Find creative, fun ways to incorporate movement into your daily life that also provide a sense of accomplishment, whether you choose walking, jogging, cycling, dancing, yoga, strength training, or participating in sports (whether organized or just a casual pick-up game).

The key is to choose activities that you actually like to do, because it'll increase the chances that you'll want to keep doing it over time.

Incorporating movement into your self-care routine doesn't have to be formal, complicated, or time-consuming. Even simple actions, like taking the stairs instead of the elevator, parking farther away from your destination to walk more, doing stretching exercises while watching TV, or having a dance break during work or chores can contribute to your daily movement goals.

Making movement a priority in your self-care routine not only benefits your physical health, but also enhances your mood, reduces stress, and promotes a sense of well-being and vitality:

- **Set realistic goals:** Start by setting realistic and achievable goals for daily physical activity. If you've been a bit of a couch spud, deciding you're going to run eight miles every day may not be realistic (or much fun). Start with something small and achievable and build up to your goal.
- **Find activities you enjoy:** Choose physical activities that you enjoy and look forward to doing, whether it's walking, jogging, cycling, dancing, swimming, yoga, or group fitness classes.
- **Schedule movement breaks:** Incorporate short movement breaks throughout your day, especially if you have a sedentary job. Set reminders to stand up, stretch, walk around, or do a few minutes of exercise every hour.
- **Make it social:** Invite friends or family members to join you in physical activities. It adds a social element but also provides motivation and accountability.
- **Mix it up:** Keep your routine interesting by mixing up your activities. Alternate between cardio, strength training, flexibility exercises, and recreational sports to target different muscle groups and prevent boredom.
- **Use everyday opportunities:** Look for opportunities to be active in your daily life. Take the stairs instead of the elevator, walk or bike for short errands, do household chores vigorously, or play with pets or children.

- **Prioritize consistency:** Consistency is the key to reaping the benefits of regular physical activity. Make movement a non-negotiable part of your daily routine, just like brushing your teeth or eating meals.
- **Track your progress:** Keep track of your physical activity and progress over time. Use a fitness tracker, journal, or app to monitor your steps, workout duration, intensity, and accomplishments.
- **Listen to your body:** Pay attention to your body's cues and adjust your activity level as needed. Rest when you're fatigued, and avoid pushing yourself to the point of pain or injury.
- **Seek professional guidance:** If you're unsure about where to start or have specific health concerns, consult with a fitness trainer or your doctor for personalized guidance and recommendations.

6. Personal Development

Personal development covers many of the areas that people typically think of as self-care. It can include restorative/relaxing practices, to develop self-awareness and mental, emotional, social, physical and spiritual growth, and may be made up of actions like reading,mindfulness, meditation, journaling, goal-setting, and daily gratitude practices. I'll cover more about each of these areas below.

Engaging in personal development empowers you to reach your full potential and enhances your confidence, adaptability, and capacity to effectively navigate life's challenges.

Here are some action steps you can take to integrate personal development into your daily self-care routine:

- **Set goals:** Identify specific areas of personal growth or skills you want to develop and set SMART goals to work towards them. Break down large goals into smaller, manageable tasks to track progress and stay motivated.
- **Set aside time:** Dedicate time each day for personal development activities.
- **Create a plan:** Know ahead of time what activities you want to do, skills you want to focus on, etc. You could read, listen to podcasts, attend workshops, practice skills, or engage in reflective exercises like journaling or meditation.
- **Practice self-compassion:** Be kind to yourself and give yourself grace. Acknowledge that personal development is a journey, and it's okay to encounter obstacles along the way. Use setbacks as opportunities for learning and growth.
- **Network and connect:** Build relationships with like-minded individuals who share your interests or goals. Join communities, attend networking events, participate in online forums or groups, and engage in meaningful conversations to exchange ideas, gain perspectives, and expand your network.
- **Stay curious and open-minded:** Cultivate a curious mindset and remain open to new experiences, challenges, and learning opportunities. Embrace lifelong learning as a fundamental aspect of personal development and self-care.

Let's dive a little bit deeper into some of the specific actions mentioned in personal development.

SMART Goals

Setting SMART goals is like making a plan that helps you succeed step by step. Each letter in SMART stands for something important:

- **Specific:** This means being clear about what you want to achieve. Instead of saying, "I want to get better at work," you say, "I want to finish a big project by Friday."
- **Measurable:** You need to know how to measure your progress. So, you can say "I want to read twenty pages of a book every day," instead of, "I want to read more."
- **Achievable:** Your goal should be something you can really do. It's like choosing a puzzle piece that fits. For example, saying, "I want to exercise for fifteen minutes daily" is achievable, but saying, "I want to run a marathon next week" might not be.
- **Relevant:** Your goal should make sense and matter to you. It's like picking the right ingredients for a recipe. For example, if you want to become a better writer, read more books and practice writing.
- **Time-bound:** Give yourself a deadline, so it's like having a finish line in a race. Saying, "I want to learn a new recipe by the end of this month" gives you a clear time frame.

When you use SMART goals, you're a captain steering your ship home. You know exactly where you're going, how far you've come, and when you'll arrive.

Reading

Reading expands our knowledge and helps us explore new ideas, perspectives, and information and broadens our understanding of the world and ourselves. Moreover, reading can relax and reduce stress and provide an escape from the demands of daily life.

It doesn't matter whether you read fiction or non-fiction, and it can be in any format: audiobook, digital, or an old-school paperback book. Picking a topic you're interested in is what really matters.

I read every night before bed. The amount of time varies - sometimes it's 3 sentences and sometimes it's 3 pages, but it happens every day.

Journaling

There's no "wrong" way to journal. You can physically write in a blank book or speak into a Notes app, answer introspective questions, or dump random streams of consciousness. One of the many benefits is increased self-awareness. By regularly writing about your thoughts, feelings, and experiences, you gain deeper insights into your emotions, beliefs, and patterns of behavior. This self-reflection helps you identify areas for growth, understand your strengths and weaknesses, and make more informed decisions.

Journaling also serves as a form of emotional release and stress management. Expressing your thoughts and emotions on paper can be cathartic, allowing you to process and release pent-up feelings, reduce anxiety, and improve mood regulation. Journaling can also enhance problem-solving skills and creativity by encouraging brainstorming, exploring different perspectives, and generating new ideas. Furthermore, keeping a journal provides a sense of accountability and progress tracking, helping you stay focused on your goals and track your personal growth over time. Overall, incorporating journaling into your self-care routine can promote mental clarity, emotional well-being, and personal empowerment.

Mindfulness

Mindfulness is the state of being present in the moment and having awareness of your thoughts, emotions, and sensations. It can mean focusing on your breath and your senses. Some benefits include lowering stress levels, improving resilience, and enhancing overall mental well-being. Mindfulness also enhances cognitive functions such as focus, concentration, and decision-making. Additionally, mindfulness promotes a sense of inner peace, acceptance, and gratitude, fostering a positive outlook on life and reducing symptoms of anxiety and depression.

Incorporating mindfulness into your self-care routine can lead to profound personal growth, increased resilience, and a greater sense of overall well-being.

Meditation

Meditation doesn't necessarily mean sitting cross-legged on a cushion for an hour. You can meditate while walking, listen to mantras, and in as little as one minute. At its core, meditation involves training your mind to focus and cultivate awareness, leading to a state of deep relaxation and inner peace. One of the primary benefits of meditation is stress reduction. Regular meditation practice has been shown to lower cortisol levels, reduce anxiety, and promote a sense of calmness and emotional balance.

Incorporating meditation into your self-care routine can have profound effects on your overall well-being, promoting physical, mental, and emotional health while fostering personal growth and inner peace.

Gratitude

Taking time each day to practice gratitude is one of my favorite self-care practices. Gratitude breeds contentment, but simply saying, "I'm grateful for what I have" isn't really practicing gratitude.

Sure, it's good to be grateful, but try going a bit deeper to really reap the benefits.

Practicing gratitude is also one of the easiest practices to fit into the margins of your day.

As soon as you get up in the morning or right before you go to bed, think of three things you're grateful for. Then pause for a moment and feel grateful for the wonderful day you have ahead of you—or the day you've just had. Setting your intentions helps you subconsciously set the tone for noticing more moments in your day.

Work at practicing gratitude in all the empty moments of your day. You can turn the radio off on your drive to work, speak out loud if it helps, and express your gratitude for the simple moments that make you smile and bring you peace.

7. The Way You Dress

Our clothes can communicate so much about us without saying a word. They can be our armor or an invitation.

There is no wrong way to express yourself. It's your style, and the key is to know it and own it.

Being confident and comfortable in how you dress is a part of self-care. Yes, you read that right. Your clothes and style are part of your self-care!

Paying attention to your clothes doesn't take any extra effort or energy, but can brighten and inspire you and others. Have some *fun* with it. I love to add a pop of color, whether I add a bright red patent leather wedge to my blue velvet blazer or a bright yellow belt to a red dress.

Do you have a signature look or piece that makes you feel unstoppable?

Wanna know a secret?

Whenever I wear my black harem jumpsuit, I can't help but do the MC Hammer shuffle and sing "Can't Touch This" in my head. I know my energy and attitude are definitely higher on those days.

Having a style of your own doesn't have to be expensive or confine you to one look.

Your style helps you:

- Dress with intention
- Have confidence
- Increase your creativity
- Feel comfortable and happy

By planning your outfits the night before you need them, you can save time in the morning and create a calmer start to your day. You also have the time to be mindful of what you choose. Some action steps to take:

- **Evaluate your wardrobe:** Start by assessing your current wardrobe and identifying items that make you feel confident, comfortable, and authentic. Donate or discard clothing that no longer serves you or doesn't fit your style or comfort preferences.
- **Dress for your mood:** Pay attention to how different clothing styles, colors, and textures affect your mood and confidence. Choose outfits that reflect your mood and empower you to feel your best, whether it's vibrant colors for energy, cozy fabrics for comfort, or professional attire for confidence.
- **Prioritize comfort:** Opt for clothing that prioritizes comfort without sacrificing style. Choose fabrics that feel good against your skin. Consider the fit and functionality of each garment, and invest in supportive footwear to ensure comfort throughout the day.
- **Express your personal style:** Use clothing as a form of self-expression to showcase your unique personality and preferences. Experiment with different styles, trends,

accessories, and statement pieces that reflect your individuality and make you feel empowered.

- **Mindful shopping:** Practice mindful shopping by making intentional and conscious decisions when adding new items to your wardrobe. Consider the quality, sustainability, and ethical practices of brands, and focus on purchasing items that align with your values and long-term style goals.
- **Accessorize thoughtfully:** Choose accessories like jewelry, scarves, belts, hats, or bags to add flair and personality to your outfits. Accessories can complement your clothing and enhance your overall look while expressing your personal style.

8. Decorate and Organize Your Home

Most of our days begin and end at home, and having a home that brings you joy and peace is a part of your self-care. Over 50% of individuals feel they are overwhelmed by the clutter in their lives.

Coming home from a long day of work isn't always relaxing when you open the door and find that your safe haven has turned into a war zone.

I get that it's not realistic to maintain a home in perfect order every moment of each day—even Marie Kondo has given up on that.

Clutter and Organization

How you organize your home can affect your sense of balance and calm.

Making time to prioritize simple systems can help eliminate the clutter that gets in the way of living your ideal life, but it's different from person to person. This may not necessarily be just things: it can also include negative energy of others, our own limiting beliefs, and being exposed to information 24/7.

Individual Differences

Everyone thrives in different levels of organization and cleanliness.

Some people focus on keeping things perfectly organized. For them, a tidy room can be soothing and increase their focus and mental clarity. They create an orderly retreat in an often disorganized world.

Others may not feel like everything has to be neat and orderly, and they feel more creative amid what might look like chaos to someone else.

Each of these people may feel the same joy and happiness about their home.

Organization can also vary across areas in your life, based on your priorities (or where you may exert more control). Maybe your work desk is super organized, but your car is a disaster of receipts and crumbs. No judgment—and neither is good or bad, as long as you feel comfortable and can remain effective in each of those spaces.

Negative Effects of Disorganization

How can you tell if the way you live aligns with what you need? Check the list below and see if these negative effects of disorganization are affecting you:

- **Misplaced items:** Frustration comes from not being able to find things. Your routine might be much smoother if you know where everything is. Imagine knowing exactly where to find items, like your keys, at any given time.
- **Wasted money:** Have you ever been in a situation where you buy something new because you can't find the item you know you already have?
- **Zapped motivation:** Disorganization can impact the amount of exercise you get, your engagement in family activities, and your general happiness.
- **Difficulty relaxing:** You feel a lot of residual guilt over what you "should" be doing!
- **Distracted, with decreased productivity:** Do you ever start one task, then get sucked into another?
- **Missed appointments:** If your schedule's a mess, you might miss appointments. You're not sure what's happening, where or on what day.(My husband once went to the wrong gym to pick up his son because he was distracted and made an assumption that his son was at his "regular" gym, when he was actually waiting at a gym across town.)
- **Overstimulated:** Our brains require more energy to focus on chaos, which can trigger a stress response.
- **Decreased efficiency and consistency of mundane tasks:** Organization can help you get tasks done more

quickly, thus increasing consistency. Getting things done consistently over time, rather than all at once, can help us find more time for other things.

It's important to recognize that a cluttered environment may visually represent inner chaos. Unfinished tasks, unresolved emotions, and a general lack of clarity can show up as physical clutter.

Taking the time to sort through your things can be therapeutic. When you give an item sentimental value, it has power—both positive or negative. You may not even recognize this until you let something go. To illustrate, hanging on to clothes you *hope to fit into someday* places a negative judgment on where you are right now.

You can also keep the memory without the item. Take a picture and intentionally put the item on display. (This is a great tip for all the hundreds of art projects your kids bring home.)

It's not always the amount of stuff we have, but how we store and organize it that can affect how smoothly our home runs. The feeling we get being there and our daily sense of balance and calm contributes to and impacts our self-care.

Do you need to get rid of your things or need better storage? You may have thirty pairs of shoes, but do you have the space and organization you need (thirty cubbies in a closet organizer, for example)? If so, then go for it.

Tips to Stay Organized

Go room by room and divide your things into four boxes: things to donate, things to throw away, things to keep, and things to store. If you don't need it or love it, consider getting rid of it. This can be an ongoing process. I have a Goodwill bag that I continually add to. When I see an item I no longer want, I can put it there and take it off my mental plate.

- **Be proactive:** Create a system to prevent the mess, rather than just clean up after you make a mess.
- **Keep a schedule:** A cleaning schedule can help you keep a clean house, especially when you have a list of "to-dos" to follow.
- **Follow the thirty-second rule:** Not to be confused with the icky "five-second rule" (which involves eating food off the ground that's been there only five seconds), this powerful rule by Sandra Felton of Messies Anonymous goes like this: If a job takes thirty seconds or less to do, do it immediately, whether it applies to putting away your shoes, sorting mail, and other small jobs.
- **Watch your "hot spots":** Remember those piles you just got rid of? Clutter tends to accumulate in the same places— the front door, the kitchen table—every day. FlyLady Marla Cilley recommends that you focus on the areas where you tend to leave clutter at the end of each day so they don't turn into big piles again.
- **Put your things away:** Once you have a place for everything, remember this: When you take something out, simply put it back.

- **Take fifteen minutes:** Many cleaning experts, including FlyLady, recommend that you put on some music and take fifteen minutes a few times a day to clean. You can get a lot done in fifteen minutes, and it doesn't impact your schedule too much.
- **Get rid of junk mail:** One simple way to cut down on paper clutter is to get rid of the junk before it comes in.
- **Don't over-organize:** Keep things broad and general, and allow for some flexibility. It becomes too stressful if things are micro-organized (like Monica from *Friends*).
- **Find a place for everything:** It not only makes it easier for you to find, but it's easier for others to know where to return things.
- **One in, one out**: If you bring something in, get rid of something. I saw someone online state that for every Amazon box that comes in their house, they fill it up with items to donate. I'm not sure if I could do that every time, but it's a nice idea, right?
- **Daily light cleaning**: Do a light cleaning at the end of every day. Some straightening of pillows, daily dishes, items for the most part back in their place—very surface level.
- **Weekly thorough cleaning**: Do a more thorough cleaning once a week (or hire someone to do it for you if it fits your budget).

How You Decorate

Creating a home that soothes your soul is not about hiring a designer or having expensive things. It's about surrounding yourself with the things you love.

Some factors that can play a role include:

- Colors and themes that speak to you can help you feel relaxed and energized. Grays, browns, and creams can help you relax, but pops of color can also ignite joy.
- Smells can affect your mood. The hospitality industry has recognized how important this is to client experience, and some hotels have begun to pipe aromas, like ice cream or rosemary into their lobbies. Fun fact: Febreze was odorless when it first came out. Sales were initially poor, and focus groups commented that they couldn't tell if it did anything, since they couldn't smell anything in their homes after they used it. The company added a smell because people wanted their house to smell fresh and clean, and sales took off.
- Set the mood and tone in your environment by creating different playlists to reflect how you want to feel.
- Wabi-sabi is a Japanese philosophy and concept that embraces imperfection, transience, and simplicity. It means that design does not need to be perfect, so value the pieces you have. Your personal touches and knickknacks can bring back nostalgic memories and make you smile.
- Pay attention to the lighting in your home—does it create warmth?

I personally love hygge (pronounced "hoo-ga"), the Danish concept of creating joy and coziness in life's everyday moments. When someone walks into a *huggelige* (hoo-ga-lee, meaning cozy and welcoming) home, they immediately get the "I'd love to live here" vibe. Hygge is a state of mind and an instant stress reliever.

It's important to keep things simple in order to immerse yourself in this carefree and cozy lifestyle. Coziness is key when it comes to hygge decor. One way to do this is by decorating with fluffy pillows and soft comforters, including layers of blankets and pillows on the couch for a warm place to unwind. You can also do this by creating cozy nooks like a window bench or loveseat. These make for a great place to relax with a good book and cup of hot cocoa for some peace and quiet.

- **Decorate with candles:** Candles are key to a hygge lifestyle. Use the soft glow of a candle throughout your home to create a warm radiance.
- **Music** can help set the tone for how you feel in your home.
- **Pay attention to lighting**: Twinkly lights are also ideal when it comes to hygge decor. Not only are they cheery and festive, but they look great everywhere. You can use them in your bedroom, living room, or even on your outdoor patio! Like candles, they give off a softer light and can add a pleasant touch to your home design without overwhelming it.
- **Texture and natural elements:** Texture may not be the first thing that comes to mind when you think of cozy hygge decor. However, introducing texture to your living space can add interest to an otherwise minimalist design. You can do this by incorporating warm, natural materials like wood and wool in your decor or add variety with flowers for a small pop of color.
- **Fireplace:** Huddling around the fire, whether outside or inside, is a huge part of Danish culture. It's the perfect time to gather with friends and family and be thankful for your

company. A fireplace is an essential element to hygge decor. It represents warmth and togetherness with loved ones.

- **Spa-style bathroom:** Instead of just using your bathroom for a quick shower in the morning, make it a relaxing retreat. Your bathroom should be a place you go to for rest and rejuvenation. To create a pleasant, peaceful bathroom, add hidden storage space to avoid unwanted clutter. For extra enjoyment, invest in candles and comfy robes for a laid-back and serene design.

Incorporating home decor and organization is a part of your self-care routine because you invest in your long-term growth and resilience.

The Bottom Line

Ultimately, self-care doesn't have to be fancy or time-consuming. You can walk, read, meditate, declutter a drawer, breathe, call a friend—the options are endless!

Start with five minutes of self-care per day. As it gets easier to fit that in, you can build to seven, ten, fifteen minutes, and even multiple times in your day. Who says it has to be done all at once?

It sounds so simple, but how often do you really take time to do self-care?

Chapter 7

Final Takeaways

We've arrived at the summit!

So, as we wrap up the last of the three pillars (Mindset, Time Planning, and Self-Care) of the Exhausted to Empowered Formula, take a moment to think about which one feels the most comfortable, such as something you already do.

Which one challenged you and may need some extra attention? Does the idea of focusing on all of them together sound like a lot? No worries—I've got you covered. Let's finish up!

In Part 1, we addressed the big picture. We started with an awareness of where burnout comes from and what it looks like (so it doesn't sneak up on you). Next, we talked about how work/life balance is not just some mythical unicorn that people talk about but no one ever sees. It's real and it's possible. Then we looked at the power of mental fitness in building our strength and resilience to help us navigate whatever life throws at us, so we can maintain work/life balance and help prevent burnout.

Like a GPS, you need to know your starting and end point to gain useful directions to your destination. Without that, you would just have some action steps but no clear direction.

Hopefully you've done some of the suggested action steps as you read through each chapter.

What have you learned about yourself? Where are you currently, and what do you need to move toward? What strengths have you underestimated in yourself or not even realized you have?

In Part 2 of this book, you learned how to achieve the lifestyle you are looking for.

I've always loved *The Wizard of Oz* (even though, as a kid, I hid behind the couch every time the Wicked Witch came on). Did you?

When Glinda helps Dorothy realize *she* had the power to go home all along, I used to think, "Well, why didn't she just tell her and make it happen?"

Like so many of us, Dorothy didn't believe in her own power and potential. We go about things the hard way, expecting some outside "thing" to fix our situation. But that doesn't create the sustained bliss you're looking for each day.

That comes from *you*!

Read that again.

YOU.

Making a Change

If you want to change something about yourself:

- Embrace change as an opportunity for growth and learning, rather than a threat. Start with small, manageable changes and gradually expand your comfort zone.
- Understand time planning: prioritizing tasks, delegating responsibilities, setting boundaries, and eliminating time-wasting activities. Also, schedule regular blocks of time for self-care, learning, reflection, and goal-setting. Investing time in personal growth is an investment in your overall well-being and future success.
- Challenge negative self-talk and limiting beliefs by cultivating self-compassion, practicing positive affirmations, and focusing on strengths and past successes. Setbacks and challenges are normal parts of the growth process and can serve as valuable learning experiences.
- Set realistic, achievable goals, break them down into manageable steps, and track their progress regularly. Use strategies for staying motivated and accountable, such as creating accountability partnerships, celebrating milestones, and visualizing success. Finally, remember your reasons for pursuing personal growth.
- Be proactive in seeking help, asking for feedback, and learning from others' experiences. You are not alone in

your journey, and seeking support is a sign of strength, not weakness.

Remember, the goal isn't to try to add all the strategies all at once.

Start with just one. Consistently.

Celebrate simple milestones instead of waiting for what you believe to be a bigger, grander accomplishment.

As you embark on your journey toward enhancing mental fitness, achieving work/life balance, and prioritizing self-care, remember that every step you take is a testament to your resilience and commitment to personal growth.

Embrace your challenges as opportunities for learning and growth, cultivate a positive mindset that empowers you to overcome obstacles with courage and determination, and prioritize self-care as a non-negotiable aspect of your well-being.

Surround yourself with support, seek guidance when needed, and celebrate your progress along the way. Remember that your mental fitness serves as a strong foundation for resilience, fulfillment, and success in all areas of life.

You are capable, you are worthy, and you are on a path to a brighter, more fulfilling future.

If you want, I can walk by your side every step of the way, working through your obstacles and celebrating your wins!

Let's make it happen for you!

Listen to me guide you on my podcast, through insightful blog posts, and reels and posts on social media like Instagram, LinkedIn, and Facebook.

Head on over to my website, www.bestdlife.com, for free resources, courses, and opportunities to have me work with you or your company directly.

No matter how you process, learn, and create new systems in your life, I want to help you. Let's hop on a free coaching call. I'll help you identify where you feel the most frazzled, and we'll find the right path together!

Acknowledgements

I want to express my deepest gratitude to my husband, Ned, and my children, Dominic and Calista, for their unwavering support throughout this journey. They graciously endured my questions, doubts, and countless revisions, always offering encouragement and a smile.

A huge round of applause goes to my editor, Melissa Brock, for her insightful feedback and dedication to shaping this manuscript into its best form.

Heartfelt thanks to my beta readers, Kristi and Mary, whose honest feedback and constructive criticism helped strengthen the story.

A special thanks to my book coach, Bev Ryan, who skillfully guided me in structuring my thoughts and ideas into a clear and meaningful format.

Finally, to you, the reader, thank you for embarking on this journey with me. By reading this, you've given yourself a true gift - the opportunity ro change you life!

Easy Artichoke Spinach Dip (here's the recipe I promised you earlier in the book)

1 Box frozen chopped spinach (defrosted)
1 Can chopped artichoke hearts (or whole hearts and you can chop yourself)
1 Cup mayonnaise
1 Cup grated parmesan cheese
1 Tablespoon minced garlic

Combine all ingredients in an oven safe pan. Heat at 350 degrees until warm throughout and serve with your favorite chip or cracker. (I personally love Tricuits and Pita Chips)

Bibliography

Administration for Children and Families. 2024. *Secondary Traumatic Stress.* https://www.acf.hhs.gov/trauma-toolkit/secondary-traumatic-stress. Accessed August 23, 2024.

Advanced Dermatology. 2023. *Study: 1 in 4 Americans Feel Guilty Pampering Themselves.* https://www.advdermatology.com/blog/how-americans-make-time-for-self-care-study/. Accessed August 24, 2024.

Atlassian. 2022. *What is Parkinson's Law and Why is it Sabotaging Your Productivity?* https://www.atlassian.com/blog/productivity/what-is-parkinsons-law. Accessed August 24, 2024.

Bankrate. 2020. *Survey: Surprisingly Fewer People Losing Sleep Over Money Issues.* https://www.bankrate.com/finance/credit-cards/losing-sleep-survey/. Accessed August 24, 2024.

BetterUp. 2022. *Are You Reaching Your Full Potential? A Guide to Personal Development.* https://www.betterup.com/blog/personal-development. Accessed August 24, 2024.

Bin There Dump That. 2024. *12 Jaw-Dropping Clutter Statistics That Will Make You Want to Declutter Today!* https://www.bintheredumpthatusa.com/article/clutter-statistics. Accessed August 24, 2024.

Bird & Associates. 2021. How to Prevent Burnout as a Result of Perfectionism. https://birdpsychological.com/adults/how-to-prevent-burnout-as-a-result-of-perfectionism/ Accessed August 24, 2024.

Business Insider. 2022. *12 Proven Ways to Raise Serotonin Levels and Boost Your Mood.* https://www.businessinsider.com/guides/health/mental-health/how-to-increase-serotonin Accessed August 24, 2024.

Business News Daily. 2023. *Why Do Employees Prefer Flexible Work Arrangements?* https://www.businessnewsdaily.com/flexible-work-arrangements. Accessed August 24, 2024.

Campuswell. 2024. *How You Can Manage Your Stress and Become More Resilient.* https://www.campuswell.com/stress-effect-on-body-build-resilience. Accessed August 24, 2024.

Clear, James. 2018. *Atomic Habits: An Easy and Proven Way to Build Good Habits and Break Bad Ones.* New York: Avery.

Clear, James. 2024. *The Habits Guide: How to Build Good Habits and Break Bad Ones.* https://jamesclear.com/habits. Accessed August 24, 2024.

Corporate Wellness Magazine. 2024. *The Impact of Employee Wellness on Organizational Culture: A Deep Dive.* https://www.corporatewellnessmagazine.com/article/the-impact-of-employee-wellness-on-organizational-culture-a-deep-dive. Accessed August 24, 2024.

David, Susan. 2016. *Emotional Agility: Get Unstuck, Embrace Change, and Thrive in Work and Life.* New York: Avery.

Dweck, Carol. 2006. *Mindset: The New Psychology of Success.* New York: Random House.

EveryoneSocial. 2024. *16 Employee Burnout Statistics You Can't Ignore.* https://everyonesocial.com/blog/employee-burnout-statistics/. Accessed August 20, 2024.

FitOn. 2024. Here's Why Sleep-Care is the New Self-Care. https://fitonapp.com/wellness/sleep-care-as-self-care/. Accessed August 24, 2024.

HelpGuide.org. 2024. Benefits of Mindfulness. https://www.helpguide.org/harvard/benefits-of-mindfulness.htm. Accessed August 24, 2024.

Gallup. 2018. *Employee Burnout, Part 1: The 5 Main Causes.* https://www.gallup.com/workplace/237059/employee-burnout-part-main-causes.aspx. Accessed August 20, 2024.

Helpguide.org. 2024. *The Mental Health Benefits of Exercise.* https://www.helpguide.org/articles/healthy-living/the-mental-health-benefits-of-exercise.htm. Accessed August 24, 2024.

Indeed. 2024. *Employee Burnout Report: COVID-19's Impact and 3 Strategies to Curb It.* https://www.indeed.com/lead/preventing-employee-burnout-report. Accessed August 20, 2024.

Intermountain Health. 2023. *Food as a Form of Self-Care.* https://intermountainhealthcare.org/blogs/food-as-self-care. Accessed August 24, 2024.

Kona. 2024. *Employee Engagement Tool.* https://www.heykona.com/solution/employee-Engagement-tool. Accessed August 20, 2024.

Mental Health Match. 2024. *How Therapy Helps You Regulate Your Emotions.* https://mentalhealthmatch.com/articles/anxiety/how-therapy-can-help-you-regulate-your-emotions. Accessed August 24, 2024.

MindTools. 2024. *SMART Goals.* https://www.mindtools.com/a4wo118/smart-goals. Accessed August 24, 2024.

Minimalism. 2024. *How and Why Nutrition and Self-Care Go Hand in Hand.* https://minimalism.co/articles/nutrition-and-self-care. Accessed August 24, 2024.

National Institute of Health. 2013. *The Benefits of Slumber.* https://newsinhealth.nih.gov/2013/04/benefits-slumber. Accessed August 24, 2024.

New Jersey Institute of Technology Human Resources. 2024. *Benefits of Remote Work.* https://hr.njit.edu/benefits-remote-work. Accessed August 24, 2024.

Pew Research Center. 2023. *More than 4 in 10 U.S. Workers Don't Take All Their Paid Time Off.* https://www.pewresearch.org/short-reads/2023/08/10/more-than-4-in-10-u-s-workers-dont-take-all-their-paid-time-off/. Accessed August 23, 2024.

Psychology Today. 2020. *5 Things People Get Wrong About Self-Care.* https://www.psychologytoday.com/us/blog/in-practice/202001/5-things-people-get-wrong-about-self-care. Accessed August 24, 2024.

ReachOut. 2024. *Mindsets.* https://schools.au.reachout.com/articles/mindsets. Accessed August 24, 2024.

Rhimes, Shonda. 2015. *Year of Yes: How to Dance it Out, Stand in the Sun and Be Your Own Person.* New York: Simon & Schuster.

Skillshare. 2021. *Nutrition as Self-Care: Good for Your Body, Mind, and Spirit.* https://www.skillshare.com/en/blog/nutrition-as-self-care-good-for-your-body-mind-and-spirit/. Accessed August 24, 2024.

Ten Thousand Coffees. 2023. *Employee Burnout: Signs, Symptoms, and Impact on Organizational Performance.* https://www.tenthousandcoffees.com/blog/employee-burnout. Accessed August 24, 2024.

Thrivemyway. 2023. *Important Burnout Stats 2024: Trends and Facts to Know.* https://thrivemyway.com/burnout-stats/. Accessed August 23, 2024.

Time Doctor. 2024. *7 Time Management Myths You Should Stop Believing Today.* https://www.timedoctor.com/blog/time-management-myths/ Accessed August 24, 2024.

Todoist. 2024. The Complete Guide to Planning Your Day. https://doist.com/blog/how-to-plan-your-day/. Accessed August 20, 2024.

USA Today. 2023. Hiding Purchases or Debts from a Partner Can Break a Relationship—or Spice it Up. https://www.usatoday.com/story/money/2023/12/10/hiding-purchases-debts-partner-financial-infidelity/71825940007/. Accessed August 24, 2024.

WebMD. 2022. Workplace Stress and Burnout: What Causes It and What Organizations Can Do to Help. https://www.webmd-healthservices.com/blog/workplace-stress-and-burnout-what-causes-it-and-what-organizations-can-do-to-help/. Accessed August 23, 2024.

Wikipedia. 2024. *Febreze.* https://en.wikipedia.org/wiki/Febreze. Accessed August 24, 2024.

Zippia. 2023. *20+ Alarming Burnout Statistics: Stress and Lack of Motivation in the Workplace.* https://www.zippia.com/advice/burnout-statistics/. Accessed August 24, 2024.

www.ingramcontent.com/pod-product-compliance
Lightning Source LLC
Chambersburg PA
CBHW070715130626
46553CB00005B/1999